BAREFOOT
AT THE LAKE

BAREFOOT
AT THE LAKE

A MEMOIR OF SUMMER PEOPLE
AND WATER CREATURES

BRUCE FOGLE

september

1 3 5 7 9 8 6 4 2

First published in 2015 by September Publishing

The lyrics for 'Lover, Come Back to Me' on page 204:
Words by Oscar Hammerstein II. Music by Sigmund Romberg
Copyrigh⌐ ⌐he Oscar
Hammerste lishing Co.
(admini renewal
copyrig :cured.

ISBN 978-1-910463-00-0

September Publishing
www.septemberpublishing.org

THE HERON

One day when Grace and I were crayfish hunting on the shore of the lake, we found a dead heron under a mighty elm tree.
'How do you think it died?' I asked.
'Of a broken heart,' Grace replied.
'That's not true. Shall we bury it?'

Grace had short hair that looked like it had been cut any old how, not cut like her sister Glory's. Glory's hair always looked like the coloured pictures in my mother's *Chatelaine* magazine. More girly. Grace had shiny brown hair and legs as straight as poplars. Her knees were chapped like a boy's. Grace's nose was neat and her face flat, and although she wasn't exquisitely beautiful like I thought her mother was, I thought she was quite pretty. Everyone has his or her own smell and Grace had hers. Like summer by the lake, she smelled of grass and gasoline.

1

*

'I want some feathers,' Grace answered.

She straightened out the dead bird's wings and they were wider than her father was tall. She grabbed several long grey wing feathers and pulled on them. They came away easily, all attached to bits of skin and flesh.

'Wash them off in the water,' I said.

'Stupid!' she replied and with her fingers she separated the feathers and left them in a row on a rock, each one with sinew and skin hanging from it.

'How should we bury her?' she asked.

'How do you know it's a girl?' I replied.

'You're so dumb! Boy birds can't be that beautiful. She's a girl.'

We walked back through the shallows to my cottage to get a trowel and spade to dig a grave for the bird, and returned the easier way, by rowboat. Now that we were both ten years old, if we wore our life jackets Grace and I were allowed to go out alone in it. Canoes tip easy but it's hard to tip a flat-bottomed rowboat. The first week at the lake we went out together almost every day.

You never keep anything in boats but there were always two life jackets, a flashlight and a bailing can in the rowboat. I untied it from the dock. Other girls at the lake always held onto both gunwales when they got in. Grace just stepped right into it. Grace was strong and rowed like a boy, not a girl. One pull of her arms and the rowboat glided fast over the lake, the bow making a little splash each time she took another pull on the oars. Whenever I was in the rowboat with Grace, she always rowed. She just did, without asking.

When I was in the rowboat with my uncle, he always asked me to row.

Sometimes when we were out together Grace would stop rowing. We liked to see how and where the wind took us. Once she said, 'Let's lie down so no one can see us.' We did, with our feet touching each other under the rowing seat.

'Do you think they'll think we've fallen overboard and drowned?' I asked.

'It doesn't matter what they think,' Grace answered.

Grace continued rowing, then stopped.

'I need to see where I'm going,' Grace said, talking to herself, not to me, and pulling on one oar and pushing on the other. The rowboat smoothly spun around. Now pushing on the oars instead of pulling on them, we continued along the shoreline, stern first, Grace looking for where we had left the dead heron. I didn't mind. It was languid and peaceful rowing that way. I turned around too and we both watched as some cattle grazing in the long steep pasture leading down to the water's edge found their way through the maze of cedar trees that lined the shore and drank the clear water.

When we returned to the dead bird, I tied the rowboat's bowline around the trunk of a cedar. By the time I had finished Grace had already picked up the heron, as heavy as one of Mrs Nichols' big old egg-laying hens, and carried its body onto the meadow grass.

'You dig and I'll prepare her body,' she instructed me.

I usually did what Grace told me to do. I couldn't dig in my bare feet with the spade, so with the trowel I'd got from the tool house I cut into the grass making a square, then I used the spade to lift the grass all the way around the square. I'd seen my father do that with a spade when he was making the vegetable patch on the cottage lawn up by the gravel road.

Grace prepared the heron. After taking some more feathers, she squeezed the wings against the bird's body and rolled it in the grass to make a neat bundle. She tried to bend the legs but she couldn't.

'Dig deeper,' she told me, after she inspected the grave and silently, without complaining, I did. Digging was easy. The black earth was as soft as cashmere. It was easier than digging through sand on the beach to find clay.

When the grave was deep enough to satisfy Grace, she placed the dead heron in it, but no matter how she tried she couldn't get its feet in. I tried to bend them but I couldn't either.

'We'll have to break them,' Grace said.

'No!' I answered. 'If you break them she won't be able to fly in heaven.'

'That doesn't matter. She won't be good at flying anyways 'cause I've taken her feathers,' Grace replied.

'You shouldn't have,' I answered. 'You give them back. They're not yours. They're the bird's.'

'No. I'm going to make an Indian headdress from them, to wear in my hair. How do you think the Indians get the feathers they wear at the powwow?'

'That's different. Give it back its feathers!' I thundered.

Grace was surprised by my sternness, so she did, laying the feathers she had just plucked, and all the other feathers that were lying on a rock on the shore, on top of the heron's body in its grave.

'Good,' I said and with the trowel I cut the grass in a long thin line around the heron's extended legs, lifted the grass and set it aside then dug out the earth below so that its legs would fit in.

4

THE HERON

When the heron was completely in its grave, using her hand, Grace pushed the black earth over it. Then she placed the turfs of grass back and stomped on them with her bare feet to make them smooth. While she did that I found an old dead cedar branch, broke it so that it made a cross and planted it on the bird's grave.

'The good Lord made you then he took you away. Ahem,' I said.

'Ahem,' Grace said, then added, 'I want to go for a swim.'

We rowed back to my cottage. Young children like us couldn't go swimming unless there were older children or an adult swimming or watching. Uncle Reub couldn't swim but he was sitting on a deck chair looking out at the lake and my mum said that it was only important that he was an adult. She said if we got in trouble he could yell for help louder than we could. The water was still cold and I didn't want to get my shoulders wet. I floated on my inner tube and my back felt as warm as an oven.

OPENING UP THE COTTAGE

There were no locks on the cottage doors. When my father built our summer home, he made three small bedrooms, an indoor toilet and bath, and everything else big – the kitchen, the combined living and dining room. Picture windows overlooked the lake, twenty feet away. It hadn't entered his mind he'd ever need locks. This was in 1949, when I was five years old, and it wasn't Toronto, it was the Kawartha Lakes a hundred miles northeast of the city, where the last strip of cultivatable farmland collided with unending primordial forest. The few farmers who tried to work this boulder-strewn land went to church on Sundays, grew their own food and, from the way the wife of the nearest farmer Mrs Nichols dressed, made their own clothing. You don't need locks when these are your neighbours.

Each year, when school finished in June, the summer people – my parents, their friends and their children – invaded Long

Point on Lake Chemong. Just as abruptly they left the lake, and the locals, at the end of August and returned to where they lived the rest of the year. Some to Toronto, others to Peterborough, the local market town seven miles away.

My father, a man with a natural majesty and a deficiency of words, made his first serious spring visit to the cottage in early April, to see what damage winter had brought. In April 1954, when my mother was in Montreal with my brother, Robert, and there was no one to look after me, Dad took me and Uncle Reub with him. Angus too. Angus was a small black dog. He had bad breath but I didn't mind that. Dogs are totally honest with you and you can be completely honest with them. More than you can with people. Bad breath didn't matter.

Except along the shoreline where we collected water for cooking, ice still covered the lake. It was too early to risk refilling the drained plumbing, there might be another frost, so we carried our drinking water in thermos bottles and used a plot amongst the trees for our toilet. Angus drank from the lake and peed where he wanted. At night it was so cold the only way I could get out of bed in the morning was by wrapping a comforter around me.

That first morning, in the living room, I found Uncle Reub by the south-facing window, already up and dressed. I watched unnoticed as my small uncle gently lifted a fly, stunned into a stupor by the night-time freeze, and moved it into the warm rays of the morning sun bursting through the window. I joined him and we both watched in silence as the warm heat revived its soul and brought it to life again.

The cottage was properly opened when we moved to the lake at the end of June. That year Uncle Reub came with us. Angus and I ran from the car straight to the front of the cottage.

Angus wanted to see if there were dead fish to roll on. I wanted to see what the lake was doing and to count how many different birds I could see on the land and on the water. There was always at least one dark, long-necked cormorant by the shore and sometimes further out on the lake a compact flock of green-winged teals. Robins busied themselves in the grass searching for earthworms, or in the trees calling to me to cheerily cheerily cheer-up cheer-up. Robins were city birds. I was more interested in the eye-catching country birds, bright orange and black Baltimore orioles, egg-yolk yellow goldfinches that I called wild canaries, belted kingfishers on willow branches overhanging the lake, red-headed woodpeckers battering their beaks in the white pines and especially my favourite but most elusive bird, the fiery red cardinal. All of those birds might live in Toronto but I never saw them there. I knew I'd see them at the cottage. Everything at the lake – the bugs, the birds, the animals, the smells, the weather, the waves, even the people – was more exciting. Angus disappeared. He'd come back when he was hungry or wanted me to rub his belly. I knew that, as old as he was, he was off hunting. He loved the lake.

Rob and I used the wheelbarrow to clear the shoreline. Dad told us to. He never said much to either of us, to anyone for that matter, but on that first day at the cottage when so much had to be done he gave us short, simple instructions. Although Dad wasn't much of a talker, Mum's extrovert nature made up for his lack of gregariousness. Dad was a doer and my older brother and I, as young as we were, both knew that physically he could do anything.

Fifty years later, at my father's funeral, after his casket had been lowered into the rich, dark soil below the hard frost line and we'd all taken turns, using his own cottage spade, shovelling frozen clods of earth onto it, Steve, my brother's best friend at the lake, asked us what it was like to have had a father who didn't say much.

'When we lived at the lake I wished my father looked like yours,' Steve said. 'Whatever he was doing, sawing wood, repairing the raft, just fishing, he was always so dignified, so handsome, so strong. I thought he was Clark Gable. But I never knew who he was. I never managed to get more than a few syllables out of him. Did he ever talk to you two?'

'No,' my brother and I answered in unison.

'He wasn't someone to talk about your feelings with,' I added. 'I had my mother or my Uncle Reub for that. Talking with my dad wasn't important. What was important was I knew that if he had to, he could kick the living shit out of anybody else's dad.'

'That's right,' my brother nodded.

On the shoreline there was driftwood, whitening in the sun, a tangled mess of early seaweed, and even though the fishing season didn't open until the first of July there was a painted, wooden fishing lure nestled in the weeds, its rusty hooks the same colour as decomposing vegetation. We watched shoals of minnows dart this way and that in the shallows then it was our job to remove the oiled tarpaulin from the canoe, raised off the ground over winter on two sawhorses, and clean the spiders' webs, leaves, larvae and pupae from inside it. I saved the pupae to unwrap and inspect later. I was good at saving the best for the last. To my ten-year-old mind the pupae were miniature Egyptian mummies, prepared by hosts of never-seen slave insects.

Rob and I did the same with the rowboat and while we were allowed to carry the canoe into the lake, our father had

Mum help him turn the heavier rowboat over and put it in the water. Rob and I both stared. Kids did things in the lake together. Not grown-ups. Uncle Reub sat on a lawn chair, a heavy book on his lap, looking out at the lake. He was one of many uncles my brother and I had, sixteen of them, almost all in Toronto. The others frequently visited but it was my mother's big brother who stayed, sometimes just for a few days, sometimes for months. It was only with us, not with his other brothers or sisters. Back then I didn't think much about why. I knew he'd been married. Twice. My father never seemed to mind, he treated his brother-in-law like a shadow. My mother would sometimes be quite stern with her older brother. She used the same tone of voice she used when she reprimanded Rob and me.

After the rowboat was in the lake, water leaked into it – at least an inch of water.

'You should caulk and paint that rowboat,' Mum said. She was always giving instructions, not just to my father. To everyone. She did so with an affable look and an alluring smile, and everyone seemed content to do as they were told to do.

'Everyone thinks your mother is sexy,' I'd heard Steve telling Rob. At that time I didn't know exactly what that meant.

'The wood will expand,' Dad replied and it did. It took only days for the leaking to stop. In mid-July my mother repainted the rowboat herself. All summer she was busy. Not complaining busy although sometimes, when I said something that pleased her, she'd say, 'I wish your father was more like you.' She was happy busy, taking us by boat to swimming lessons each Tuesday, laughing with the other mothers as they lay together on their lounge chairs each afternoon, talking about I don't know what, collecting potatoes from kind Mrs Nichols at the farmhouse at the top of the hill. On rainy days she read stories to all the children on the point and taught us how to play poker. In my mind my father was the colour of the land, brown and green. My mother was the colour she painted the rowboat, fiery red.

After the canoe and rowboat were in the lake, Dad went into the boathouse and using chain winches thrown over the ceiling beams he lowered the motorboat back into the water. Dad got the motor out of the tool house, took its casing off, blew in it, cleaned the carburettor, put in a new spark plug, then, without putting the casing back on, carried the motor close to his broad chest to the boathouse, stepped into the boat, hung the motor from the transom, tightened the wing nuts, then pulled the starter cord. More fiddling with the carburettor and another pull and he was surrounded by blue smoke and unmuffled noise. He replaced the casing, then put the motor in reverse and backed the boat out of the boathouse. Once he was clear he throttled forward, slowly at first, and then, after the spluttering stopped, full throttle. With a boyish grin on his face he made tight turns, so tight that water came over the gunwales and he had to throttle back fast or he'd capsize. My father didn't swim and he never wore one of the Kapok-filled life jackets he always had us wear.

Dad built the cottage himself. Until the previous summer it was the last one in a row of twenty other cottages on the point, with a field next to it where Mrs Nichols' three black-and-white dairy cows had grazed.

Dad used two-by-four-inch pine for its frame and six-inch-wide cedar planks for its clapboard siding. He sanded and shellacked the cedar sidings each spring for the first three years then last year gave up and painted it all brilliant white, like the other cottages at our end of the point. Uncle Reub was with us when Dad did that and while watching my dad prepare the cedar sidings, he walked over to where my father was and ran his hand gently over the knots and veins of the rich wood. Uncle Reub's hands were small and soft, like a fat girl's.

'Your cottage was once alive and your father is showing his deep respect for it. It lived in the woods, over there by the lake,' he said.

He turned towards the ancient cedars that shaded the spearmint and raspberries that had seeded themselves in the new hedge my family had planted.

'They gave up their lives so that your father had wood to build your home, so you could be safe here in your own cottage during the summer. And when you come back here each June it comes alive again.'

Sometimes I didn't understand what my uncle was telling me but I always knew that even if I didn't understand, it was – somehow – interesting.

Our next-door neighbour's cottage had green windows and doors and the one next to that, Grace and Glory's, had red ones, so to be different my father painted his windows and doors a deep, dark cobalt blue. Under the relentless summer sun, the cobalt had now turned to a soft powder blue.

At the end of June the water in the lake was still too cold for me to swim in, but once we finished our chores Rob went for a dip. He was a better swimmer than I was. Mum had promised him that he could try for his Royal Life Saving Society Bronze Medallion this summer. All I had was my Red Cross Junior badge.

Using a pump from the tool house – my dad's storage cabin – I inflated a car tyre inner tube and floated on it. I didn't mind the cold on my legs when the sun melted my back.

'Chicken!' Rob spat as he surfaced near me and splashed me with cold water.

'I'm going over to Grace's,' I shouted to my mother.

'Not in the water, you're not, unless Robert goes with you,' she called back from the front of the cottage where she was pushing the rotating-blade lawn mower across the long grass. Uncle Reub had moved his chair onto the dock to get out of her way. Like Angus, Dad had now disappeared.

'I'm not going with Robert,' I replied.

'Then get out of the water and walk over,' she said.

I did. Grace was more fun than Rob.

CATCHING CRAYFISH

I peered over the side of the boat, looking for the flat rocks I knew crayfish hid under. My father used crayfish for fishing for bass, pickerel and muskies. Grace rowed. In the rowboat we could go far down the lake, farther than we would ever go if we walked in the shallow waters along the shoreline. Less than 500 yards from our cottages a grove of cedar trees had collapsed in a storm into the lake. It was too deep to walk around them and there was too much poison ivy on the ground around their trunks to get past on land. In the rowboat we were on a new adventure, visiting a part of the lake past the fallen trees we had never visited before.

Looking through the calm, clear water I saw small circles of clean rocks and knew that's where fish – rock bass, I'd been told by my uncle – had spawned just a few weeks before. He had told me that this is how fish made their homes attractive for their partners and said that's what my mother did with the cottage. Close to shore I spotted unending flat rocks in the shallows and told Grace to row to the shore. We tied the rowboat to a tree and went hunting.

'Walk slowly,' I commanded. 'Don't scare them.'

Grace knew how to do this. She was as good at catching crayfish as I was. All these rocks were just perfect. We both knew that but neither said so out loud. In slow motion Grace lifted one end of a flat rock off the bottom without causing a ripple on the lake's surface and there it was, a perfectly camouflaged crayfish, the colour of limestone and sand. My father had shown all the children on the point how to catch bait, worms at night by muffled light, minnows in minnow traps under the dock and crayfish under rocks. Slowly, like Mr Everett's brown dog stalking a rabbit, she put her hand into the lake and lowered it towards the crayfish, then in a flash with her thumb and her forefinger she grabbed it behind its claws and pressed it to the bottom of the lake. When she was sure it couldn't bite her she raised it out of the lake and showed it to me. Its big claws swung back on both sides, trying in vain to hurt her.

'That's too big for fishing,' I said, but she kept it anyways and put it in the rowboat.

I was pleased with Grace, even proud of her. None of the other girls in the cottages on Long Point ever wanted to go crayfish hunting, but she always did.

We decided to work in opposite directions, me on one side of the rowboat and Grace on the other. Silently, with bent backs and eyes close to the water we looked for flat rocks lying on other rocks, places where crayfish could hide from us, and those rocks were everywhere. Just about every rock we lifted had a crayfish hiding underneath and within a short time the rowboat was crawling with dozens of irritated crayfish. In their anger some were biting others. Each time another was thrown into the rowboat, the nearest crayfish raised its opened claws. In the white bottom of the boat they looked like a congregation of praying scorpions in a dry desert.

After a while Grace got bored and walked to the shaded shore where she sat on a large rock between two great cedars that leaned out over the lake. Behind her was a meadow of summer flowers, airy and shimmering and light, gently dancing to the soft south wind. I could see that no one had ever walked through that meadow. 'I wonder whether this is what heaven's like,' I thought. On the shoreline spring storms had washed away soil from around the trees' massive chocolate-brown roots and peering out from within those roots Grace saw two tiny eyes.

'Get the flashlight,' Grace ordered, but I knew I couldn't. It wasn't there.

Rowing at night shortly after we arrived, Uncle had broken our shared silence by saying, 'Let's throw the flashlight into the lake.' I was disturbed by the suggestion. I didn't want to. The flashlight had made me feel safe and, besides, it was my father's.

'I'll buy another. Turn it on. Let's throw it in the lake and watch what happens.'

I turned it on. Holding it in both hands, not really wanting to throw it in the lake, I asked my uncle, 'How long will it shine?' and my uncle, smiling a broad grin, said, 'Long enough to entertain all the fish in the lake. Then, when it's served a purpose, when it's had a reason for living, it will go out.'

I liked that answer so I gently placed the flashlight into the water and watched as it twinkled into the deep. For a moment I had an impulse to follow it, to see what lived at the bottom of the lake.

I didn't tell Grace why the flashlight wasn't there, I just said, 'It's not here,' and quietly walked over to where she was.

'I can't see anything,' I said.

'Stupid! It's your fault it's gone.'

'It's not my fault. Anything would run away just looking at you!' I hissed.

Sometimes Grace was like Angus. She didn't think first. She just said things or did things. That made me angry and I said things I didn't really mean. We both decided not to talk to each other ever again and to go back home.

Rowing back to the cottage – with Grace rowing because she said so – the army of angry crayfish marched this way and that on the bottom of the boat, all their claws raised in anger. Grace rowed squatting with her feet beside her. I sat backwards with my feet over the transom. That boat filled with crayfish was just too thrilling and it didn't take long for Grace to speak.

'Mr Muskratt says that crayfish are tasty and we should eat them.'

'When did he say that?' I asked. Mr Muskratt lived up the lake, on the Indian Reserve. He was thickset and strong. His leathery face was the colour of the woods. Even his dark brown eyes blended into the landscape. He never said much, almost nothing at all. 'Yep.' 'Nope.' 'Eh?' when he wanted you to say something again.

On Friday, when he came in his canoe selling fish, he saw the crayfish my dad had for fishing and told him that instead of wasting his time fishing with them, my dad should just buy Mr Muskratt's fish and eat the crayfish instead. He said that Mrs Muskratt sometimes boiled them and sometimes roasted them for Mr Muskratt and their children.

AN EARLY SUMMER DAY

Sometimes, even when you're little, you know when life is perfect. You just know. The sun woke me up early and it dazzled off the white clapboard siding on the back of the cottage. It was so clear and it was so bright it almost hurt just to keep my eyes open. Warm rain overnight had left the grass heavy with wet and the black soil in the vegetable patch near the gravelled road steamed.

It was my second week at the lake and so far it only rained at night. I walked round to the front of the cottage. The lake looked like an enormous puddle of mercury and it gave such a pure reflection of the cloudless morning sky and the forested shore on the far side I couldn't tell up from down. When the water looked like that I knew that nothing would happen. Fish wouldn't bite. Ducks wouldn't fly. Only dragonflies enjoyed that nothingness. I wasn't surprised my uncle was there, motionless in a lawn chair only yards from the shoreline facing the lake. He was always looking out at the lake. Sometimes he'd sit there in his pyjamas all day until my mother would tell him to get dressed. This time I wondered whether my uncle had died during the night and I was the only one to know.

I didn't move. For a long time I just stared, watching to see if he was breathing but somehow he knew I was there.

'I've been looking down towards the bridge. It's too far to see now but when cars had their lights on earlier, they looked like tiny fireflies slowly gliding across the water.'

He paused and again we were both silent. That wasn't unusual. Sometimes Uncle Reub let his silences stretch out and I didn't mind that.

'What do you think of this morning?' Uncle eventually asked but I didn't answer. I knew what I thought. I knew a lot but I didn't always talk about it.

'I'm going to frog bog,' I finally said, not as an answer but as a fact.

'With Robert?'

I never did anything with my big brother. If we played together we ended up fighting. We had the same parents and lived in the same house but that was the extent of our shared togetherness.

'Just me.'

We both looked down the lake, me straining to see a car crossing the bridge, then to my surprise my uncle said, 'May I come along?'

Uncle Reub didn't do much at the cottage. He didn't swim, or even put his feet in the lake. He certainly didn't take walks on his own like my mother did. He didn't seem to care much about his clothes. During the first week at the cottage he wore city trousers held up by braces, over a white shirt. Now that it was hotter and more sultry during the day he wore a white undershirt. This morning he was in trousers but still wearing his pyjama top. He always wore black leather city shoes, usually with white socks. To me, my uncle seemed separate from other adults. He listened to me and I was pleased with that attention. I said, 'Yes.'

Frog bog was part of the dead forest, the part that lay in the lake. I thought there once must have been a great battle with an evil spirit that lurked in the depths of the lake and that the trees gave up their lives and drowned themselves to save their friends in the living forest. Maybe it was just a shooting star that had fallen on them. Most of the trees were cedars but there were willow trees too. I knew that because, out of all that death, some of the fallen trunks had green shoots emerging from them and on those shoots were magical new willow leaves. Each year the muddle of fallen branches and trunks seemed to get more complicated. They sank deeper into the bog, nestling in each other's arms. This is where I came to catch tadpoles and frogs, painted turtles and water snakes.

Uncle Reub sometimes told me stories when we were alone together but today we walked in a mutual solitude, across the dew-damp lawn, up to the gravelled road that ran behind the cottages. My bare feet were already tough. I never wore shoes when we lived at the cottage, except when my family took me to a restaurant or to a movie in town. Shoes were for city boys. Even on the hottest days, when tar melted on the road to Bridgenorth, I only ever experienced a satisfying warmth in my bare feet that made me feel I was connected to the land, that I understood it, that it was part of me.

We walked up the point, past silent cottages where not a single curtain was yet drawn. In the fluorescent yellow light of early morning, all the cottages looked and smelled as if they were freshly painted. They probably were. I was only a boy but

I understood how proud the cottagers were of their summer homes. Each garden was perfection, lush green lawns, pink granite stone and concrete pathways from the gravel road to the cottage door, petunias and begonias in a constellation of marshalled perfection. It was as if the cottagers challenged the wild around them, that they vied with each other to be the best at taming the surrounding forest.

Passing Dr Sweeting's clapboard grey cottage, a dog barked and a wiry brown mink darted from the stand of white pines the cottage nestled in and across our path. I was glad Angus wasn't with us. He would have killed that mink. We walked on in a complicated silence until the road and the cottages ended and the woods began.

'Is this your secret place?' Uncle Reub asked.

I thought that was a childish question but I didn't say so. It wasn't a secret. Everyone knew where the living woods and the dead forest were.

'It's the woods,' I answered.

We followed a track that all the children on Long Point and Cedar Bay had made, through the maple and birch trees, down to the lake. 'That's frog bog,' I told my uncle, pointing to the shambles of tree trunks, branches, weeds and reeds that lined that deep and hidden bay on Lake Chemong.

Uncle walked to the edge of a bank of sweetgrass and looked out over the stillness. I sometimes did that too. In its quiet and calm that scene, that view of the rushes and reeds and the forested far shore of the lake and the turquoise sky, that picture, even to me as a young boy, was perfection. I looked at my uncle standing there, as still as a totem pole, and for a moment I thought he might suddenly march forward right through that sweetgrass into the sparkling still water – without taking off his shoes or rolling up his trousers – that he might forge a path through the pickerel weed and water lilies then let them close together behind him. But he didn't.

'I didn't know there was sweetgrass here. I bet muskrats think this is paradise.'

'I'm going over there,' I replied.

I walked along the straight trunk of one fallen cedar tree and then another out into the marsh, to an open pool of clear water. Along the southerly shoreline of the bog, bulrushes were all standing to attention, their tops like thin little bear-skin hats on skinny green soldiers. The water lilies were all shut tight. They wouldn't expose their hearts until the sun was much higher. Later in the summer, if all of July was hot and humid, the water in the pond would get covered in bright green algae but now, in early July, it was crystal clear and you could see absolutely everything in it. Streamlined silvery minnows were easy to see but if you looked harder there were tiny, long slender dragonfly larvae that looked like they'd got baby leaves stuck to their tails. At the edges of the pond that's where the tadpoles were.

Uncle walked slowly along the same fallen tree trunks. I thought he looked quite ridiculous, with his arms straight out to keep his balance, like Christ on the cross, I thought. He reached where I was and joined me where I was kneeling on a stump looking into the water.

'Is it interesting, what you're looking at?'

I knew my uncle couldn't see what I saw. Grace and Perry, Steve's younger brother, could but grown-ups couldn't. Giant water bugs were stabbing the tadpoles to death. It was scary to watch and I didn't like it but also I did like it and always watched.

All that my uncle saw were iridescent green dragonflies, like phosphorescent toothpicks, hovering over the pond, and on the water, long-legged water striders skating gracefully over the surface, never sinking.

'Are you wondering how those insects can walk on water?' my uncle asked.

Other grown-ups never knew what was in my mind but my uncle sometimes did. I really wanted to know why the water bugs were so mean to the tadpoles but I'd also wondered why water striders didn't sink when they stopped skating.

'They're lighter than water so they don't sink.'

I thought for a moment.

'But ducks are heavy and they don't sink either,' I said, not so much as a question but as a fact.

'You're right. Good thinking. What ducks do is they trap air in their feathers. The trapped air makes a duck lighter than water and that's why a duck doesn't sink. I really should have explained it better. Water striders do the same as ducks. They trap air on their legs just like ducks trap air in their feathers. Shall we catch one and see?'

On his knees on the log, balancing himself with one hand, Uncle Reub reached down to the water, trying to grab a water strider and show me its legs. As he leaned out over the pond his glasses case, in the breast pocket of his pyjama top, slid out and plopped into the water. It sank almost immediately, just like the *Titanic* I thought, raising its stern to the sky before dying. Uncle pulled himself upright and rested on his knees. It was easy to see his glasses case, shiny and silvery, nestling in the black leaves and guck a few feet away at the bottom of frog bog, but I could see the concerned look in my uncle's eyes.

'I've got my shoes on. Can you go in and get it?' Uncle asked.

'No,' I replied, not because I couldn't but because I didn't want to get into frog bog.

Uncle Reub paused for a while then said, 'OK then. Let's see if we can fish it out.'

He walked back along the logs, this time faster, with his arms more like you'd expect from a grown-up, over to a willow tree and took a knife from his pocket. Grown-up men all carried penknives in their pockets. My father's penknife, in his pants' pocket whether he was in trousers in the city or shorts at the cottage, was made from brown tortoiseshell and had two blades that my dad kept razor sharp with a small pumice stone. Black electrical tape kept the tortoiseshell from falling off. My uncle's knife was completely different. It was a small single blade, thicker than a penknife, three inches long with a horn handle. The blade was in a soft tan leather sheath covered in white and red and black beads. I thought it was the most wonderful knife I had seen.

With that knife, Uncle Reub cut two green branches from near the trunk of a willow so that both were the same thickness and each had two fingers at their ends.

'When I practised general medicine in Mandan, North Dakota, a good friend of mine showed me how to do this. What we'll do is get the ends of these branches under each side of the case. They'll act like two forks and we'll slowly lift it up and out of the water.'

Uncle and I walked back along the tree trunks. First we acted as a team, with me pushing one branch under one side of the metal case and my uncle doing the same with the other, but each time we tried to raise the glasses case the branches bent too much and the case slid back into the black leaves and stirred up the guck at the bottom of the pond. Or my uncle and I couldn't coordinate what we were doing and the glasses case slipped back to its murky home. Uncle tried using both branches himself but with no success, and now the water was so murky it was almost impossible to see where the glasses case was. I wanted to give up and go home. When I was young I found that easiest to do. My uncle knelt on the tree trunk. He was a small man and sometimes reminded me of Humpty Dumpty but now he looked even smaller and I felt sorry for him.

'Are you sure you can't get it for me?' Uncle Reub asked.

I felt embarrassed. I was in my bathing suit. I loved the lake. There was nothing better in the whole summer than floating in hot sunshine buoyed up by the warmth and the strength of a truck or car tyre's inner tube. But getting into the bog was scary. I didn't mind the goo on the bottom. In fact I liked the squishy feel. I didn't mind the frogs or painted turtles either and the water snakes always hid when Grace or Perry got into the bog, but there were snapping turtles in there too and the year before I was bitten when I caught one. It was horrible. I was carrying it back to show Grace and hadn't noticed that the snapping turtle's head had slowly emerged and turned upside down over its back. At the instant I saw this the snapper crushed its jaws into my forefinger. It didn't let go until I put it back in the bog and it swam off.

I never talked about that. I certainly wouldn't have told other adults but Uncle Reub was different so I said, 'I'm frightened of the snapping turtles.'

'They are frightening. You're very sensible. Now I've got these sticks and I've got my knife, and Edgar, my friend in Mandan, taught me how to throw it. I can knock the right eye out of a rattlesnake at ten paces with this knife so if you get in there, I promise, nothing will come near you. You're safe with me.'

The sun was higher. It was almost nine o'clock and I felt its warmth heat my bare back. With my uncle's assurance I slid off the log until my feet felt the mushy bottom of the bog. The water was colder than I expected and came to the top of my bathing suit. My shoulders lifted and I squeezed my arms against my sides.

'You don't even have to look at what you're doing. We're a team,' Uncle said. 'Now, open your fingers and bend your body over to your right.'

I obeyed. In slow motion I leaned over to my right, reaching down towards the bottom of the bog until my whole arm and shoulder were in the water. I didn't like what I was doing but I said nothing.

'Over a bit more. Now forward. Keep your fingers open. Down. There. Can you feel it?'

I could. I grasped the case, together with some leaves as black as coal, and, still not smiling, raised it all out of the water and handed everything to my uncle, who opened the case and emptied it of water. I hoped there'd be a tadpole in it, stabbed to death by a water bug, but there wasn't. Now, standing up, I felt warmer, and quite satisfied with myself. I actually felt like going for a swim but I climbed out of the pond, onto the log and with my uncle walked back to the shore.

Before we left the woods for home, Uncle cut a handful of sweetgrass with his knife.

'The next time your father makes a barbecue, let's put this on the embers,' he said.

'Will it make the hamburgers taste better?' I asked and my uncle replied, 'Better than that. The incense from this sweetgrass will relieve us all of our weariness. And yes, the meat will taste better too.'

We walked back through the trees and just before the gravel road and cottages on Long Point became visible, Uncle Reub said once more, 'Hold on for a moment.'

Again he took his knife out of its beaded sheath and deftly cut two bands of bark off one of the surrounding birch trees. 'When we get back we'll soak these in water. I'll show you how to make an unsinkable birchbark canoe.'

By the time we got back to the cottage, my family was already having breakfast. 'Where'd you go?' Robert asked me.

'Nowhere,' I answered.

'What were you two doing this morning?' my mother asked Uncle Reub.

'Not much,' replied her brother.

'You're not going to tell us anything?' Mum asked.

'Brucie and I were discussing the meaning of life,' Uncle Reub answered.

I smiled inside me. I loved that we had a shared secret. We finished our breakfast all together, white toast, butter tarts and milk.

THE CANOE

The slapping rain was sudden and passed in minutes, leaving a rainbow over the still lake. Grace and I found my uncle inside the cottage talking quietly to my mother who, when we arrived, left and went to her bedroom.

'I've just finished making the canoe,' Uncle Reub said.

I had been surprised that my uncle had promised to make me a model canoe. I was more used to seeing him just sit in his chair or read a big book. Uncle Reub had found an aluminium bucket in my father's shed and filled it with water to soak the white bark he had cut from the birch tree near frog bog. I had watched him make some slits at both ends with his knife and bend the bark in half with its woody side out, not its bark side as I'd expected, but before I could ask why I got bored and left to find Grace.

'Do you hear how shrill that woodpecker's cry is?' my uncle had asked. 'A storm's coming.'

And in not much longer than it took that storm to come and pass, the miniature boat was finished.

'Folks, that stitching at the bow and stern, it's called whip-stitching. When I used to patch up people at The Mayo I used something called mattress stitching but this is better for boats. Both of them make the seal watertight. Along the gunwales where I've bound in sweetgrass, those are called simple stitches.'

I was impressed, especially by the two thwarts my uncle had whittled with his knife, to keep the canoe firmly spread.

'Will it float like our canoe or just tip over?' Grace asked, and my uncle replied that we should take it out on the lake and find out.

Grace and I wanted to go in the big red canoe – we were allowed in it with a grown-up – but Uncle Reub said it was too wobbly for him to get in and out so we all got in the rowboat. Angus was on the dock asking to come but Grace said he had to stay at home.

'I row,' said Grace, so she did, with me in the front and Uncle in the back.

As she rowed, my uncle leaned forward and said to Grace, 'Do you know where all the flowers go when winter comes?'

'They all die,' she answered.

'That could be true,' Uncle replied. 'But I have a friend who thinks differently. He says that God would never let such beauty die. He says all the flowers go to heaven and come back next year to make rainbows.'

'If God decides all the flowers come back, what does he do with the birds?' I asked.

'That's difficult to know,' my uncle answered. 'Our Jewish religion tells us that each year God decides who will live and who will die. My friend Edgar's religion says that nothing ever dies forever, that everything comes back in one way or another.'

'Is Edgar a Christian?' Grace asked as she continued rowing.

'You know, I don't exactly know what his religion is,' Uncle replied. 'Edgar is a Lakota Sioux medicine man but he's a modern thinker. He goes to church but he also believes in his people's ancient customs.'

'I'm going to frog bog,' Grace said and we returned to silence.

The lake was perfectly still as we glided past Grace's, Dr Sweeting's and all the other cottages, each nestled amongst the cedars that lined the shore. Some women had returned to their front lawns and were quietly getting on with their chores. Their motorboats remained silent in their boathouses, their row-boats, sailboats and canoes tied to their glistening, wet docks.

Grace and I had rowed to frog bog before but could never get into its still ponds. A canoe would be able to get through the pickerel weed and bulrushes and fallen trees but our rowboat with its fixed oars was too wide. Grace let the bow of the rowboat nestle into the bulrushes. 'The canoe will look good here,' she said. Uncle leaned over the side of the boat and gently placed the birch bark canoe on the water where it immediately rolled over and floated on its side.

'The bark is heavier on that side,' Uncle Reub explained. 'I can shave it down with my knife but ballast is best.'

'What's ballast?' I asked.

'Ballast is anything heavy. The grain or lumber or iron ore that Great Lake ships carry acts like ballast and keep those ships stable. If a laker doesn't have a good load on it, even it can tip over in a strong wind.'

Uncle Reub reached into his trousers pocket where he had put some gravel. He put five pieces in the canoe, lowered it over the side of the rowboat then, with the model floating on the surface of the lake, moved the gravel around until the canoe was sitting absolutely straight in the water.

'There now. Perfect. Should we leave it here, to embark on its own voyage, or take it back to the cottage?'

'Leave it here,' we said in unison. Without speaking to each other we both knew we wanted to return the next day to see where the canoe had gone.

'Let's leave it over there,' I said, pointing to a narrow channel through the bulrushes, so Grace rowed over and Uncle Reub placed the canoe where it would be washed by the wind into one of the quiet pools in the lagoon.

'It's best to get back now,' Uncle said. 'It's almost lunch-time.' And Grace turned the boat and rowed back towards the cottages.

'My friend Edgar, who says that flowers come back as rainbows, he says that those pebbles in the canoe will protect it from harm.'

'Why do you listen so much to Edgar?' Grace asked.

'That's a profound question, Grace,' my uncle replied. 'I can only answer by telling you that I had forgotten what a wise man Edgar was, until this spring when he came all the way from North Dakota to see me. It was Edgar's wise words that encouraged me to come and stay with Bruce's mother.'

'How can pebbles protect a canoe from harm? They're just pebbles,' I asked and my uncle's thoughts returned to the canoe.

'Our religion teaches us that only people have souls and it's our souls that go to heaven, but Edgar says everything has a soul, even a pebble. He says that's what will protect the canoe, the souls in those pebbles.'

'My father says that type of talk is nonsense,' Grace said, as she pulled on the oars.

'He might be right but, Grace, no one yet knows,' Uncle replied.

He paused for a while, looking at the cottages we slowly rowed past then he spoke once more.

'Edgar calls his god the Mighty Spirit. Doesn't that sound wonderful, the Mighty Spirit? He says the Mighty Spirit ensures that everything has a soul but to my mind it's those pebbles acting as ballast that protects the boat.'

Uncle Reub paused once more, then looking beyond Grace to me in the front of the boat he continued, 'Bruce, you're ballast for your mother.'

My mother was always telling me how she felt, especially about other people. I knew what Uncle Reub meant.

When we arrived at the dock and after we tied the rowboat to it and got out, Grace turned to my uncle and said, 'Can we go back tomorrow?'

SHOPPING IN BRIDGENORTH

There was a rhythm to summer life. Patterns. The Silverwood's Dairy truck delivered milk to the cottages on Long Point early each weekday morning. The milkman wore white pants, a white shirt and a white peaked cap. The Browns' Bread deliveryman arrived an hour later, the driver in a muddy brown uniform the colour of a chocolate bar wearing a peaked cap the colour of a muskrat's head. Angus would announce their arrival. Dr Sweeting's son, James, delivered the Peterborough Examiner just before supper. James was old enough to drive, but late each afternoon he bicycled the two miles into Bridgenorth to pick up the newspapers then bicycled back to deliver one to each of the cottages on Long Point. When it rained hard, Mrs Sweeting collected the papers for him. Sometimes she drove James down the point on his delivery round. Mrs Nichols brought us fresh eggs each Monday. We had swimming lessons from Mrs Blewett at her family's lumber mill in Bridgenorth every Tuesday afternoon. Mr Everett, the grumpy farmer who owned all the land around the Nichols' farm, collected garbage from the cottagers every other Thursday. He didn't like children. Best of all, the fathers arrived Friday night while children slept. Fathers meant more cars and cars meant we went places we didn't go during the week. That's what fathers were for. Mothers were for everything else.

My dad had brought fresh meat from the butchers in Toronto until Mum discovered how tasty meat was from the General Store in Bridgenorth. 'Imagine. This chicken lived within squawking distance of Bridgenorth,' she'd say as she prepared it for the oven. 'My mother killed her own chickens. Isn't that dreadful? We had chicken each Friday. She went to the market and chose the chicken she wanted, took it home and wrung its neck. I had to watch. Then she cut its head off and held it upside down. Imagine. Then she said a prayer and swung it around in the air. There was blood and feathers everywhere. It was terrible. Such superstitions.'

'Why did she say a prayer?' I once asked.

'It certainly wasn't for the poor chicken,' my mother replied.

'She was thanking God that we had food on our table for the Sabbath.'

'Do you thank God for food?' I asked and my mother smiled at me, came over and pressed me hard to her chest.

'I thank God for you,' she answered.

On Saturdays Dad sometimes drove us to Peterborough, for supper at Fosters Restaurant on George Street. Some of our Peterborough neighbours on the lake had stores on George Street. Mr Silver had a shoe store, Mr Collis a men's clothing store, Mr Cherney a furniture store, Mr Yudin the theatre. Their children were either a few years younger or older than I was. I saw them when we went swimming out to our raft and at swimming lessons each week but we didn't search each other out to play with. Not until we were a lot older and understood the sustaining worth of shared, warm memories.

At our end of the point, early on Monday mornings the fathers all left to return to Toronto, leaving the mothers with us. Our family had only one car so when my mother wanted to go to Bridgenorth during the week, to shop or pick up mail, we went in our red-bottomed fourteen-foot cedar boat with its fourteen-horsepower Evinrude motor.

The milkman and the bread man had both come and gone. Rob was at Glory's cottage and I was searching through the stony gravel by the shoreline, looking for the roundest and flattest stones to skip across the lake's still water. Angus, lying in the grass, was watching me. I hoped that making stones skip as many times as I could might make them flatter but I was interrupted by my mother who asked if I wanted to go to Bridgenorth with her.

'I'll have a cigarette then we'll go,' she called from the cottage porch.

The lake lay listless, shrouded in a heat haze. The water by the shoreline was warm, almost hot. I walked through it and with each of my steps, grey clouds of lake bottom swirled up to the surface where it just lingered. A school of jet-black, baby catfish darted away in all directions then, as if drawn by an invisible magnet, found comfort in each other once more and moved on.

Across the lake a mile away, a single cotton candy cloud cast its shadow on the hills, then onto the lake itself. When the wind was blowing, I sometimes watched a cloud's shadow cross the lake and would run down the point and up to the highway, just to see if I was faster than the sky itself. Today, I shuffled around on the shore playing with seaweed. Others thought seaweed was smelly and dirty but I was intrigued by it. A single strand of lake weed was as soft and as fragile as a strand of cooked spaghetti but when it was torn by storms from the bed of the lake and twisted and tied by the lake's waves it became stronger than my father.

Outside, on the cottage terrace, my mother lit her Black Cat cigarette and looked out over the lake. I knew that I shouldn't speak to her until her cigarette had burned to its cork tip. This was her quiet time.

My mother always checked up and down the lake before taking the boat out. If there was a wind developing, even if it wasn't strong, even if there weren't any whitecaps, the shopping trip was cancelled. Today the lake was calm. She took from the wall her pencilled list she had tacked there, put it in the pocket in her shorts and walked with me to the boat.

'Reub, put this cardigan on if you get cold,' she said to her brother as she stopped by the lawn chair where he was sitting, a heavy book resting on his lap, unread.

In the boat she lifted the gas tank and gave it a shake: she never blithely trusted the arrow on the fuel gauge. If it was low we would stop at the marine gas station at the Blewetts' lumber mill.

Mum and I put on our Kapok-filled life preservers. Hers was like a vest with ties in front. Mine slipped around the back of my head, down my chest and tied at my waist. In her short shorts and tight blouse and wearing her padded life vest, I was aware of how my mother's arrival in the village always attracted the attention of the local men in Bridgenorth. At the age of ten I didn't understand how exotic, how alien and how sexy she appeared to them. I don't know whether the other young 'city' mothers had the same effect on the local men. They probably did.

On a calm day like today it took no more than fifteen minutes to reach the bridge, then only five minutes more to get to where the boat could be beached. Mum talked to me most of the way but what with the engine noise I didn't hear much. There was no dock to tie up to, so Mum always approached the beach at a good speed then cut the motor and lifted the propeller out of the water, allowing the boat's momentum to drive us far enough onto the beach for her to hop over the bow onto the sand without her getting her feet wet, then tie the boat's bowline to a tree while we walked up the steep dusty road to the general store at the top of the hill.

Bridgenorth had all the necessities of cottage life and no more. A general store, a post office, Mr Bell's gas station, a bait shop that also sold grilled sandwiches, an ice house, a barber's shop with a pool room the children were not allowed in, and a machine shop. My mother had a Bridgenorth shopping ritual. We never visited the ice house. Collecting sawdust-covered lake ice for our kitchen icebox, where my mother kept her meat, fish and dairy and my father kept his fishing worms, was left to my father to do on weekends. Her first visit was to the post office, to collect that week's mail and read whichever letters couldn't wait until she returned to the cottage. 'Now she's going to ask the postmistress about her children,' I thought and as always she did. Then we'd visit the general store, to stock up on the raw materials of life, soap suds, powdered cleanser, matches, spare fuses, forty-eight ounce tins of tomato juice, packets of Freshie and Kool-Aid, popping corn, sewing materials, oil for the lamps. Shopping always took a long time. There were others in front of us, summer people but also local people from Bridgenorth and the surrounding farms, and no one was in a hurry. There wasn't much more than polite talk between the summer people and the local people although my mother, always smiling, always asking questions, talked to everyone.

Somehow I knew the local people were unlike my family and my friends. They looked different. Paler. Less animated. They didn't seem to smile much. Their clothes were old although on Sundays when they went to the white clapboard or red-brick churches in Bridgenorth they dressed in dark suits and dark dresses. It seemed to me they came from a separate world and lived in their own muted solitude.

I enjoyed going shopping. There were no shops in Toronto like Bridgenorth's general store, where someone served you and where you could buy just about anything, but now I was getting bored and was happy to leave. It was hot. I wanted to get back to Grace and the cottagers and go with Perry to our fort in the woods.

At the bottom of the hill, Mum untied the boat, told me to get in and to sit by the motor, then she pushed the boat off the beach into the lake, hopping onto the long bow deck at the very last moment. She paddled far enough out so that she could lower the propeller, then she pulled the starter coil, put the motor into reverse and backed out until it was safe to put the motor into forward, swing around and head back out into the lake. It wasn't safe. The propeller hit a rock and the shear pin on the propeller broke. Only our momentum now carried us forward.

Mum cut the engine, lifted the propeller out of the water, rotated it with her fingers and knew exactly what she had done. In the freshening westerly wind she paddled the boat back towards the cedar-lined shore. In the shallows she got out into the water and with a pliers from the fishing-tackle box, removed the flexible safety pin, took off the propeller, removed the broken shear pin and inserted another, one of many spares kept in the tackle box. My mother lowered the propeller back into the lake and got in the boat.

'I bet Grace knows how to change a shear pin,' she said.

THE SWIMMING
LESSON

Grace's mother drove her daughters, Rob and me to our swimming lesson the next day. The sky was threatening and there was a chop on the lake. My mother knew it was best not to venture out in the boat on days like that.

'I don't want to go,' I told Mum.

'If it's too rough to go swimming, Mrs Blewett will teach you artificial respiration instead,' she replied. 'She will never put you in any danger.'

I wasn't worried about danger. On a steely cold, blustery day I didn't want to get into angry, rough water.

Steve and Perry were already at the marina. Mrs Blewett arrived and she was in her bathing suit. That meant we'd have to go swimming.

When my father built our cottage, Earl Blewett's sawmill just north of the bridge in Bridgenorth was still active, sending its trucks over the frozen lake in winter to collect timber harvested during the summer and fall from the few remaining first growth forests around the interconnected finger lakes of the Kawarthas. Dad bought the cedar cladding for the cottage from Mr Blewett. Uncle Reub told me he thought the Blewetts could be descendants of the very first white men who came through Lake Chemong with Samuel de Champlain in the seventeenth century, that their real name was probably Bleuet, the French word for both cornflowers and blueberries. That was exciting. That meant my swimming teacher was in my school history books.

Now the sawmill was less active. Mr Blewett couldn't compete with the prices at Beaver Lumber, where cheap pine from British Columbia was sold, so he retired his tug and added a marina and marine gas station. We hoisted our fourteen-foot cedar Peterborough boat up to the rafters of our boathouse for the winter, but cottagers with more valuable boats were starting to store their boats at the Blewetts'. These were hand-made twenty-two-foot mahogany Shepherds, built 200 miles away in Niagara-on-the-Lake, or even more expensive mahogany Chris-Craft, built in Algonac, 300 miles west, across the St Clair River in Michigan. The sawmill owner's wife, May Blewett, pumped gas at the dockside gas station and also gave weekly swimming lessons to the summer children. At the end of each August, if we passed our tests, she dispensed Red Cross and Royal Life Saving Society pins with our names engraved on them.

Mrs Blewett was older than our mothers, in her forties, and always wore a white bathing cap when she swam. All our mothers, especially Grace and Glory's, were small and slim.

Mrs Blewett had the robust shape of the local women, a large chest and an equally large bottom. She was what my mother called 'buxom'.

'It's fresh today so we'll practise artificial respiration on land then towing in the water,' she told us. 'Pair up everyone,' and we did so with people we were comfortable with, Grace with Glory, Perry with me, Steve with Rob.

'Do you remember what we learned last week?' she asked. 'Put your victim on his side, open his mouth and remove any seaweed. Then onto his front and press your hands firmly just below his shoulder blades so you hear him breathing out. You'll be doing this to each other so get going now.'

Before Perry said anything I decided I'd be the victim, lay down on my stomach and put my hands under my shoulders, so Perry had my elbows to pull on when he was told to do so. Perry was almost a year older than me but we were the same height. His mother didn't cut his curly light brown hair all summer and by the time we returned to Toronto at the end of August I thought he looked like a girl.

'Ready, children? Rescuers, keep your hands flat and press firmly on your victims' backs to expel water from the lungs.'

Perry pressed hard and quietly, and involuntarily I expelled air from my lungs. Rob pressed on Steve's back and Steve emitted a really loud, exaggerated moan. The other boys in the class all laughed.

'This is not a laughing matter!' Mrs Blewett told him. I thought it was like being back at school and that wasn't right. It was summertime and we were free to do whatever we wanted to, especially never wear shoes.

'Now pull back on your victims' elbows to make them breath in good air.'

Perry pulled my elbows up towards him. It didn't do anything to my lungs but I intentionally breathed in, loudly.

'Bruce, you are not on stage in Toronto!'

Mrs Blewett's bare feet were inches from my head. 'If you don't take this seriously you will never learn how to save a drowning victim.'

Perry kept pressing and pulling and, having nothing else to do, I thought about how I would do this to Angus. Then we switched and Perry was the drowning victim.

Rhythmically I pressed on his back then pulled on his elbows. It was fun and I wondered whether next week I could practise on Grace instead.

After we finished attempting artificial respiration we sat in a horseshoe on the grass while Mrs Blewett told us how to break loose from a drowning victim who has grabbed you, then tow him to safety.

'Steven, come here so I can demonstrate how to break a death grip.'

Grinning back at us, Steve went over and stood behind Mrs Blewett. Steve was fourteen years old, the oldest of us. His hair was curly like Perry's but darker. Although he was much shorter than my brother, who was already almost six feet tall and catching up fast with our dad, whatever we did Steve made all the decisions. Rob had light skin and freckles. He burned easily. Steve already had a good tan, but not as good as mine. I never burned. It took only a single sunny day to turn me the colour of the inside of a Caramilk chocolate bar.

'Grab me tight around my neck,' she told Steve and he did so.

'No! Tighter!' she said and now he pressed himself firmly against her back.

Looking at us sitting in front of her, with Steve behind her she said, 'I'll do this quickly first then in slow motion so you see how to break the victim's death grip.'

Her hands came up to Steve's arms around her neck and suddenly Steve let out a high-pitched howl and his arm was in an arm lock.

'Shit, la merde! You broke my arm!' he exclaimed.

'No I haven't. It just hurts a little,' Mrs Blewett replied.

'Now in slow motion I'll show you what I did.'

'Are you going to hurt me again?' he asked.

'No. This is a slow motion demonstration.'

Once more Steve went behind her.

'There's something on your neck,' he said, wiped it off then wrapped his arms around her throat once more.

'Children, when a drowning victim puts you in a death vice this is what you do.'

In slow motion she grabbed one of Steve's hands with one hand and the elbow of the same arm with her other, then pushed up on the elbow while pulling down on the hand. Steve theatrically released his grip and, with the grace of a trained ballerina, Mrs Blewett pirouetted around behind Steve and put his arm in an arm lock.

'With your one hand keeping the victim in an arm lock, use the other to cup his chin while you tow him to safety,' she explained to us.

After practising this on each other we were ready to practise in the lake.

During our lesson the weather had got bleaker. There were whitecaps on the water and Mrs Blewett told us that as the weather was now so bad she would demonstrate towing on the shore side of the landing dock, rather than the lake side where we usually had our swimming lessons. The water was just as cold there but much calmer. All she needed was a volunteer to be the rescuer and Steve suggested Rob who, showing how manly he was, immediately dived into the water. Mrs Blewett used the new aluminium ladder to gently descend into the lake, all the time explaining to us how to tow properly.

The class, around twenty of us, all boys except for Grace and Glory and Mr Yudin's daughter, Sandy, and two girls I didn't know, lined up on the edge of the dock while Mrs Blewett grabbed Rob from behind and he broke her vice-like death grip, swung her arm into an arm lock, cupped his hand under her chin and towed her slowly past all of us. Mrs Blewett's blue bathing suit was coming undone, her chest looked like two white archery targets with big red bullseyes. None of us said a word, not even the girls.

'I'll tow you back once more,' Rob suggested and making a tight U-turn he towed her back past us, her enormous and amazingly white breasts breaking the water with each scissors kick of his legs. Mrs Blewett realised her bathing suit had come loose only when she started to climb the ladder from the lake and quickly tied the strap behind her neck.

'Mrs Blewett went skinny dipping the way you do,' Grace told her mother as she drove us back to the point.

'I don't think so, children,' her mother replied.

'She did. Her knockers are enormous.'

'Where did you hear such a word?' Grace's mother asked, and Glory told her how the strap on Mrs Blewett's bathing suit had come undone.

'How did that happen?' she asked.

'Steve told me it had partly come undone and I tried to tie it back when I towed her but that might have made it worse,' Rob offered.

'I think you boys are growing up too fast,' Grace's mother said as we arrived back at her cottage.

THE ROCKY SHOAL

ake Chemong is long and narrow, with few islands and fewer shoals, although there are dangerous rocks just below the lake's surface near Perry's cottage on Cedar Bay, about a mile up the lake – beyond frog bog. The day after our artificial respiration lesson it was sunny once more, but not too hot and humid. Perry and Steve's mother had invited my family and Grace's family for lunch. That wasn't unusual. Perry's parents always came to the Saturday night parties the cottagers on Long Point had. Perry's father hadn't built their cottage. In fact no one else's father had built their cottage except mine. They'd all been built by builders.

The families went to Perry's by boat, the fastest way. Only children walked along the lake from Long Point to Cedar Bay. At the far end of Long Point was the dead forest and adults didn't like walking through it. Up by the road was an abandoned barn and from there through the woods to the lake was private property. When you emerged from the woods the ground was wet and boggy and the air filled with mosquitoes, although at night the mosquitoes were joined by fireflies. After that there were three tarpaper shacks where poor people from Europe who didn't speak English spent their summers. The shacks were no more than four walls and a roof with a round aluminium chimney vent up the outside wall of each one. The roofs were made of red asphalt tiles all covered in lichen. I don't know who built them first but the people living in them repaired them each year, nailing over-lapping rolls of new tarpaper on the outside to the simple shack frame, floor to roof. It was easy to see what was fresh and new and black. Old tarpaper went slate grey in a year. The tarpaper shack cottagers got their water from the lake and shared an outhouse you could sometimes smell even from frog bog. Fronko, the same age as me, lived in one of those shacks and every now and then went to our fort in the woods. Adults got to Cedar Bay by walking up the hill to the county road, then along that road to the narrow lane that led back to the lake. That took at least half an hour. The boat trip took only a few minutes.

My mother drove the boat with Angus in the bow. He liked to be lookout. As she neared Perry's cottage she slowed it almost to an idle and asked us to look in the water for rocks. She didn't want to shear another pin on them. I saw the rocks first and guided my mother away from them to our landing at Perry's dock.

We had lunch together on the lawn and after lunch Perry and I went down to the lake and waded out to where the water was up to our waists. With our feet we felt the sand for clams. It wasn't long before we had dozens of them. Our families didn't eat them. We only ate fish with scales on them, but Dr

Sweeting loved these clams almost as much as he loved the catfish we caught but were too frightened to take off hooks.

Uncle Reub watched us and, out of the blue, Perry asked him why there was that rocky shoal near here but nowhere else.

'Well, that's interesting,' Uncle explained.

'You see, long before the summer folk came to Lake Chemong, long before Farmer Everett's ancestors cut down the forest and cleared the boulders from the land alongside the lake, for his corn and pigs and cows, long before the Bleuets became the Blewetts, an Indian hunter lived here. His name was Albert Gonquin although his good friends called him Al, Al Gonquin.

'Al had a beautiful daughter, Minnemoosah, and all the young men in his tribe were in love with her and asked Al for her hand in marriage.'

The other children all knew that my uncle was a great story-teller. I thought that he enjoyed telling his tales as much as we enjoyed listening to them. Mum sometimes reads us stories, especially on rainy days when we were tired of playing cards, but my uncle told stories. We never knew whether they were for real or whether he made them up as he told them. One rainy day, when Mum had gone shopping in town with Grace's mother, and Perry was visiting and my uncle had been left to look after us, he emerged from his bedroom with a tomahawk in his hands and a twinkling look of worry in his eyes. 'Men and women,' he said, 'we're under attack from Indians!' But we knew he was making that up. He told his tale anyways and today, on the front lawn of Perry's cottage, he continued.

'Now Al couldn't decide which brave should marry his daughter so he set a competition. Whoever threw the heaviest stone the farthest into Lake Chemong would marry her.'

Grace grinned and pushed me with her hands.

'Boys, the day of that competition wasn't a calm day like today. It was a rough day, a hellish rough day. The sun was shining in the sky, shining with all its might. It did its very best to make the day seem smooth and bright but the North Wind was howling down the lake and the whitecaps were taller than the tallest brave in Al's tribe. The braves threw stone after stone out into the lake but because of those waves no one could tell exactly which was the heaviest that had landed the farthest. From dawn until dusk those strong braves threw rock after rock into the lake until they had thrown so many stones that that shoal of rocks just down from your cottage had grown in height to where it is today.'

My uncle continued, 'Al Gonquin was now in a pickle. He'd promised the hand of his daughter in marriage to the brave who threw the heaviest stone the farthest but no one knew who that man was and now Minnemoosah entered the picture. She was a bit like your mother, Brucie, small, sensible, feisty, a good woman but with her own mind. "Fearless Father," she said, "it's my life and I'll decide who I marry," and right then and there she chose a brave brave named Mikkimoosah.'

'What happened to them?' Grace asked.

'Well, Al moved up north to Haliburton and named a park after himself, the braves all moved up to Mud Lake, where the Reserve now is, and Minnemoosah and Mikkimoosah moved to California where they went into the movies.'

Grace's eyes danced and she clapped her hands until they hurt.

'Tell me another!' she implored my uncle.

'Would you like to hear a true story told to me by Edgar Ten Fingers?'

'Yes! Yes!' Grace answered. Glory also gave an affirming nod and our mothers smiled.

Perry and I were more interested in doing rather than listening. We decided to see what was happening at frog bog.

THE GANG'S HIDEOUT

Nothing much happened at frog bog. There were no snakes or snapping turtles to try to catch. Perry and I parted, each going to our own cottage, but we decided to go to our fort in the woods the following morning. After breakfast the next day, as I left the cottage, I saw my uncle sitting in his chair with tears in his eyes. I didn't like seeing grown-ups cry. I didn't think they should. I thought he should go someplace else if he wasn't happy but I didn't say that. Instead I asked him if he wanted to come to the fort with me.

My uncle and I had sometimes continued to walk together and when we did we both felt comfortable in each other's company. We might walk in silence but I knew there was always something in my uncle's mind, something just beyond the reach of his telling, but whatever it was I never knew. I shared his silence with a relaxed ease. I shared my father's silence too when I went somewhere with him, but when he was silent I knew he had nothing to say. I thought he didn't think much. My uncle's mind was always working. Earlier in the summer I'd wanted to know what was weighing on it, but now I felt comfortable in my uncle's privacy.

As we walked up to the paved road we smelled skunk and saw one dead by the side of the road. Others pinched their noses when they smelled skunk but my uncle and I went to look. Uncle Reub prodded it with a stick.

'It must have just been killed. It's still soft and it hasn't bloated up yet.'

Using his foot to hold its tail in place, he cut it off with his knife and kicked the tail into the chicory growing on the side of the road.

'Why did you do that?' I asked.

'To a hungry animal a skunk looks innocent, waddling around, looking after its own business,' Uncle said. 'It doesn't need powerful muscles. Instead it surprises its enemy with its stench. I'll collect that tail when we return. It's beautiful. It might come in handy.'

'Mum won't let you,' I commented.

'I won't take it to the cottage. I'll borrow some of your mother's gin and store it in it. The smell will be gone in a week.'

We crossed the paved road then continued down a short dirt road and into the forest. Last summer, in that forest, not far from an abandoned railroad line that once went from Peterborough to Lake Chemong, I had discovered a pile of pine logs, each one around four inches thick and ten feet long. They had been there for years, I thought. I told Dad and on a spring visit this year, when the clearing in the woods was blanketed by trilliums, the two of us collected them. Dad and

I carried two at a time back to his station wagon until we collected enough for Dad to build a magnificent tree house with a floor and ceiling and two walls in the giant willow tree on their front lawn. Uncle Reub now enjoyed that tree house. Once, I heard him calling me but he wasn't in his usual lawn chair overlooking the lake. I looked up and my uncle was in the tree house, leaning over the railing, in his white undershirt and black city trousers but with thin branches of willow leaves, like a hula skirt, tucked all around his belt.

We walked silently deeper into the woods through a grove of cedars with thick brown trunks like massive Havana cigars. That part of the forest had an aromatic smell, a bit like tobacco. Then we reached a grove of birch trees where it was lighter and cheerier. Perry, Rob, Steve and I had stripped off bark from most of the trees, to write messages to each other. We had carved our names in some of the birch trees and each year our names got larger.

We reached the sugar bush and amongst the stand of maples were three lonesome wind-buffeted white pine trees, the tallest of all the trees, and all of them leaned east, away from the lake. Beyond the sugar bush was a clearing, covered in poison ivy. I was always careful but my bare leg rubbed against some of its leaves.

'Brucie, come over here.'

My uncle crushed and rolled two burdock leaves in his hands then rubbed the juicy plant over my legs.

'This burdock's an immigrant, like your great grandparents,' he said, as he rubbed the leaves on my ankle. 'They arrived from Russia eighty years ago but this plant arrived with the Pilgrim Fathers on the Mayflower and you know, it's just about as good as any medicine for stopping the itching from poison ivy.'

'How do you know that?' I asked.

'Edgar Ten Fingers told me,' Uncle answered, 'although once you've got itchy pimples, fish blood is good. You let it dry and it stops the itching.'

'Why is he called Edgar Ten Fingers?' I asked.

'And why are you called Bruce Fogle?' my uncle replied. 'It's simply his name.'

The forest got darker again until deep in the woods we reached a place where even in the driest summer, even when it never rained, the black earth never dried. In that private jungle the air was soaked in a delicate damp smell. This was where our fort was.

My uncle and I crossed a stretch of greasy earth on planks us boys had taken from cedar fences, and arrived at a place where all summer the sun never shone. Here lived snakes and birds and small animals we never saw anywhere else. When Perry and I lay on the ground and were perfectly still we could hear scurrying feet. Once, only once, I saw an owl sitting on a branch right above me. I was interested in it but it wasn't interested in me. I'd once found deer antlers, whiter than Pepsodent toothpaste, and they were now in my father's tool shed.

Our fort in this no man's land, was, we were sure, beyond anywhere anyone had ever been. That's what we thought. As soon as we arrived at the lake each summer, Perry and I, Rob and Steve visited our fort, raised ramparts, built defences, stocked up on candles and made ready for attacks. Steve told us what to do and he and Rob did most of the work. He told us we lived in the Dominion of Canada but this was our very own Dominion of Boys. I was good at doing what I was told to do and even when I wasn't strong enough I kept trying. Perry got tired easily and when that happened he gave up. No one was ever allowed to visit our fort, especially girls, not even Grace. Now I had brought my uncle.

Deep in those woods there were many skulls scattered in the leaf mould and litter, tiny little skulls that once housed the brains of the snakes we had captured and killed the year before and hung around the fort to prevent other boys, or witches, from coming near. Pinching stag beetles ambled across the brown ground and we caught them and stuck them on our arms, pretending their pincers held together war wounds. When Fronko, from the tarpaper shacks, followed us from the lake to the fort in the woods, he did so silently, without uttering a word. He just as silently let us apply Noxzema skin cleansing cream to his nose and keep him in the fort's jail until we released him to go home for lunch.

Perry, Steve and Rob were already at the fort when I arrived with Uncle Reub and they didn't know what to do or what to say when they saw him.

'Hello, boys. So this is your hideout,' he said and they nodded.

'What's this?' he asked, and with his right hand he collected a spider's web from amongst the branches that made up the fort. He divided the web into two portions and, like a sideshow magician at the county fair, he placed a portion of the web in each of his nostrils. Then he sneezed into his hand and opened it up and there was the spider that had woven that web. The other boys decided it would be fun for Uncle Reub to stay.

UNCLE'S STORIES

'Boys, it's an honour for me to be allowed to visit your fort,' Uncle Reub said, and Steve, the oldest, replied the way he thought he should. 'And it's an honour, Rob's Uncle, to have the great storyteller visit us.'

Rob showed our uncle around the fort, Perry's and my section, Rob and Steve's section and the jail where we sometimes kept Fronko. Uncle told us he was impressed by its construction and by the number of dead snakes and frogs hanging on Rob and Steve's section. The frogs had pine needles stuck in their eye sockets and through the webs of their feet.

'Were these frogs alive when you stuck them with pine needles?' Uncle asked, and Steve told him they were.

'I stick needles into people but always to make them better, never intentionally to hurt them,' Uncle replied, and he continued, 'animals can't speak up for themselves so it's up to us to do what's best for them.'

At the fort, the older boys made all the decisions, what we would use for building material, who would do what work, how we would kill the snakes we caught. Perry and I did what we were told to do, especially me. I never complained. When once I told Uncle Reub that the big boys were bullies, my uncle said that strength doesn't come from your arms and legs. Strength starts in your head then it spreads slow but sure to the rest of your body.

'Boys, now I don't mean this as criticism but do you ever think when you're here that you're acting like animals?'

When he said that I felt my uncle was criticising us but before I could speak he continued, 'You know, the animals in the woods, when they look at you they think you're very strange. They think that it's much better, it's more noble, to be an animal than to be a person.'

'There aren't many animals in the woods,' I replied. 'Besides, it's our woods.'

'Ah, but there are, and they're all watching you, right now. Everywhere. You might think this is your woods but it's really theirs. When the summer is gone and you're back at school, they will visit your fort and piss on it and make it theirs again. Do you want to know why?'

'I think we're going to hear one of Uncle's stories,' Robert said. We sat on the ground while Uncle sat on the trunk of a fallen tree.

Then he continued.

'Animals think, "People have no tails so how do they keep their feet and noses warm?"

'They see we have no hair on our bodies and wonder how we can protect ourselves from thorns and poison ivy.

'They see we only have two legs and wonder how fast we can run.

'They see we have small ears and they're not on top of our heads and they wonder how well we can hear.

'They see we have tiny noses and wonder how well we can smell.

'They see our eyes are close together and wonder how we can see danger coming from beside or behind us.

'They think we're not designed very well and that all in all it's better to be an animal.'

'Is that it?' I asked. 'Is that the story? Your stories usually start a long way further from the finish than that.'

'When do you go for lunch?' Uncle asked, and Robert answered, 'Not until lunchtime.'

'All right then. Now, boys, this is a true story,' Uncle began. 'When I lived in Mandan, as you know one of my patients Edgar Ten Fingers was an Oglala Sioux medicine man and I heard this story from him. Edgar and I were very good friends. We came from different cultures but Edgar and I saw eye to eye. He called me a "right man" and that was a great honour. I told him about the medicines I used and he told me about the medicines he used.'

'Why was he called Edgar Ten Fingers?' Steve asked.

'Steven, Bruce just asked me that very question and you know I never asked him,' Uncle Reub replied. 'Indians can have many names during their lives. That was his name when I knew him ten years ago in Mandan and it's still his name today, although if I were to choose I'd rename him Edgar White Man Healer.'

'Why?' Rob asked.

'Because his words can be more powerful than shock therapy. Now let me tell you about the medicines he used. Those pink flowers your mother grows around the cottage, those coneflowers? The Sioux smear their hands in coneflower juice when they use their bare hands to fish out dog heads from stewing dog meat.'

I wondered if Uncle's story would be about dogs but it wasn't.

'This is a story about how bountiful this land is, how it really belongs to all the animals that live on it. We think it's ours to do with as we wish, but it's really only ours to share,' Uncle began. 'The Sioux have great patience and their stories are very long. In the winter, storytellers go on for days telling a story.'

'What if someone has to go to the bathroom?' Perry asked.

'I'm sure the storyteller will pause for pee breaks,' Uncle replied, 'but as well as being very long, just like life sometimes their stories go off in different directions to where you think they're going and the story you're waiting to hear the ending of doesn't end. It just sort of peters out.'

I thought I understood what my uncle was saying. Sometimes I'd plan to do something – catch worms – but soon after starting I'd get distracted and do something else.

'Now then, boys, this Ontario forest is rich in life but in North Dakota where I lived the land was different, it was barren and empty. Two brothers, Luke and Jacob – they were really Indian spirits but let's call them brothers – were passing through North Dakota one day, where nothing much grew and there was no water to drink and in that desolate land they met a starving rabbit that asked them why they were there and where they were going.

'"We're going to Lake Chemong, in Ontario, where there's plenty of fresh grass and herbs to eat and water to drink," Luke told the rabbit. "Do as you please but you'd do well to follow us."

'Well, that rabbit told the other rabbits and they told their friends, the gophers and groundhogs, prairie dogs and field mice, that Luke had invited them to go where there was lots of grass and bugs and herbs and water. These animals told their friends and they told all the big, gentle animals, the moose and deer, caribou and reindeer, antelopes and elk, mountain goats and bighorn sheep and they all took their families and followed Luke towards the rich and fertile land around Lake Chemong.

'A timber wolf saw them all passing and asked an elderly deer why they were all travelling together and where they were going.

'The old deer said, "There will be a great feast on the shores of Lake Chemong, where there's every type of food to eat and plenty to drink. A truce has been declared during that feast and no animal will harm any other animal. The feast will last for many moons, for so long that even you and I will live happily together without any worry or care. It would be wise if you joined us."'

'Wait a minute,' said Steve. 'The deer said a truce has been declared but that's not what Luke told the rabbit.'

'Excellent, Steven. You will make a good courtroom lawyer. But let's hear what happened next. Well, that timber wolf told his friends, the coyotes and weasels, pine martens and foxes, raccoons and skunks, wildcats, bobcats and wolverines, what he had been told. And these animals told the beaver and musk-rats, otters, mink and polecats, and they all took their families and travelled together with the old deer, following Luke to Lake Chemong.'

'Did Edgar name every single animal that ever existed?' Perry asked, and Uncle answered, 'Edgar Ten Fingers says it is a great sadness if a man is not given the opportunity to finish telling his story.' And he continued.

'A painted turtle saw them as they passed and asked one of the muskrats why they were travelling together and where they were going and, Perry, he told his friends the snapping turtles and salamanders, frogs and toads, snakes and lizards, and each of these told their friends and they took their families and travelled together with the muskrat.'

'This sounds like Noah and the Ark,' I said.

'Very good,' Uncle Reub replied. 'Every religion has a Noah and the Ark story, not just ours. This story may be as old as the Noah's Ark story but it's not from the Torah.'

He carried on, 'A bear saw them as they all passed by and asked one of the frogs why they were travelling together and where they were going, and the frog replied as you'd expect the frog to reply. He said, "Luke says there will be a great feast on the beautiful and fruitful shores of Lake Chemong, that the Mighty Spirit has declared a truce amongst all things that breathe, and there will be unlimited food for us to eat and fresh, clear water to drink, forever."

'The bear is a very wise animal, the wisest, and he asked the frog one more question. "Did Luke tell you this?"

'"No," answered the frog, "but the painted turtle told me that's what he said."

'The bear asked the painted turtle, "Did Luke tell you there will be a truce amongst all those that breathe and a great feast on the shores of Lake Chemong?—"'

But before Uncle Reub could tell us what the painted turtle said we heard Grace calling, 'Uncle Reub! Mrs Fogle needs you. Angus has been shot by a porcupine!'

We all stood up. I felt a shiver go through me. Grace had run the entire way from the cottage and was breathing hard.

'What happened?' I asked Grace.

'I don't know,' she answered. 'Your mother came and told me to find you and your uncle.'

'What's happened to Angus?' I asked again.

'He's crying and won't let anyone touch him. The porcupine needles are all over his face.'

'Grace, go back and ask Mrs Nichols where her vet is. Get the vet's address and telephone number and take it to your mother. Tell her we'll probably need her to drive us there,' Uncle instructed and Grace raced back ahead of us.

'Robert and Steven, go ahead of us and see what you can do but don't touch the dog. I don't want you to end up at Civic Hospital with dog bites. They'd have to give you rabies serum.'

Rob and Steve ran ahead of us while Perry and I accompanied my uncle who moved faster than I ever thought he could. When we got back to the cottage, Angus was lying on the living room rug, panting heavily, with porcupine quills hanging around his eyes and mouth. Some quills were lying on the floor, the ones he'd managed to pull out himself. My mother was on her knees beside him, with Grace's mother looking over her shoulder. No one spoke a word.

'Angus!' I said, but he didn't even look at me.

'Aileen, has he had his rabies shot?' my uncle asked his sister, and she said he had.

'Wrap him in a bath towel?' he asked, and my mother did so. Angus let her.

'I've removed quills from people. They're like fish hooks.'

He looked carefully at Angus's face but didn't touch my dog.

'They're so close to his eyes and I think he's also been shot in his mouth. It's best we have a vet remove them.'

Grace's mother told us she had gone to Mrs Nichols, used her phone, and the vet was at his animal hospital, which was near the fairgrounds on the far side of Peterborough.

'May I come?' I asked.

With Angus lying on my mother's lap, wrapped in a beach towel, me beside them and Uncle Reub in the front, Grace's mother drove us to and through Bridgenorth, then on to Peterborough, down George Street to the far side of the city, past the fairgrounds to the Peterborough Animal Hospital.

'What will the vet do?' I asked and my mother looked at me, put her hand on my head, smiled and said, 'He'll make Angus better.'

There was no one else in the sparse, green waiting room when we arrived, but the vet heard his door open and came out to meet us. He was older than my father, with wrinkled skin the colour of my baseball mitt. His thinning brown hair was greasy and he had a toothpick wedged in his lower front teeth. His tan-coloured overalls were stained with manure. I didn't like him.

'So this is the dumb jerk who thought he was a match for a quill pig,' Dr Smith said, and he asked us to follow him into the next room. We did.

'Ma'am, leave him wrapped and put him on the table.'

My mother followed the vet's instructions.

'What is your plan of action?' Uncle Reub asked, and Dr Smith replied, 'To check out the damage then make the little bastard feel a whole lot better than he does now. I can see there are some in his mouth.' As he spoke, he filled a glass syringe with a light yellow liquid.

'I'm a medical doctor, an eye, ear, nose and throat special-ist,' Uncle Reub continued. 'Do you mind my asking what you're using?'

'Not at all. Nembutal. Same as you use. I'll give him a shot IM, wait ten minutes until he's asleep, then get those mouth quills out.'

Uncle Reub turned to me and said, 'IM means into a muscle. The injection works faster if it's given in a muscle instead of under the skin.'

He turned to Angus.

'OK now, little buddy. A quick prick and you'll be better in no time.'

Angus yelped when the vet injected the liquid into his hind leg and sure enough he was soon asleep.

The vet rolled the toothpick around in his mouth then turned to me and said, 'Son, come round here and I'll show you how to remove quills.

'Damn lucky. I've had to remove eyes from some dogs but your dog's are OK. What's his name?'

'Angus,' I answered.

'Angus, my dumb friend. We'll have you back chasing wildlife in a jiffy. Now this is what you do when I'm not around and you have to remove the quills yourself. First of all cut 'em short if you can, around an inch. They're less likely to break if you do that. At home, use needle pliers to pull them out. Give each one a quick jerk. I'll use this haemostat. All it is is a small needle pliers.'

The vet cut the needles short and starting with the ones in Angus's mouth pulled them out, one by one.

'Your turn,' he said and handed me the instrument.

'OK, son, grab the quill with the haemostat then lock it. You'll feel it click shut. Feel that? Now like you've just hooked a bass jerk it out. Fast. Good, son. Good. You're a fast learner. I can have a smoke while you remove the rest.'

I did, until all the quills were out. Angus snored.

'Do you mind if I have a cigarette too?' my mother asked. Grace's mother joined her and soon the vet's operating room was a fog of fumes.

After I'd finished Dr Smith cleaned the small punctures inside and outside Angus's mouth then said, 'Now the bad news. Young Angus here is going to sleep until tomorrow then he'll have one hell of a hangover, and the damage is fifteen bucks.'

'Money well spent. Aileen, let me pay the vet,' Uncle said.

'Sir, if this is your dog it's ten dollars. Professional courtesy,' Dr Smith added.

'And if you have an eye, ear, nose or throat problem,' my uncle replied, 'I'm at my sister's cottage at Lake Chemong. Aileen, can you leave Mrs Nichols' telephone number with the vet?'

Driving back to the cottage, I told Mum I didn't like the vet at first but now I did. I told her I thought vets only put dogs down. That's what the vet did to Perry and Steve's dog.

'Vets are medical doctors just like I am,' Uncle said, before my mother could reply. 'The big difference is I have only one species to look after. They have all the rest, livestock, pets, wildlife. Did you see he had manure on his overalls? Before he made Angus better he might have been delivering a calf. Do you know why he had a toothpick in his mouth? Because now he's going on a visit to see a robin with a broken leg and he's going to use that toothpick as a splint.'

My mother and Grace's mother both smiled.

Angus lay limp on my mother's lap, snoring loudly as we drove back through Peterborough and then through the fields and forests to Lake Chemong. Then I remembered.

'You didn't get a chance to finish your story,' I said to my uncle and he replied, 'Remember how I said that Indian stories start in one direction then sometimes veer off in a completely different direction? That's what happened today. The story started about all animals trying to live peacefully together. The bear was going to take us in a different direction. You might think he was going to remind us we should always check on stories we're told – to get news straight from the horse's mouth, but in fact he was going to be a bad bear, a jealous bear who resented that all the animals were following the rabbit. He was going to tell them that he was king of the forest and they should all follow him.'

'What happened?' I asked.

'What happened is that instead of a make-believe story you lived a true story today. When Angus needed you, you helped him and made him better.'

As we reached Long Point Angus started to blink his eyes. It took two whole days until he was able to jump back onto my bed, two whole days before I could stop worrying about him.

NEW
NEICHBOURS

Each calm, blue day summer got prettier and prettier. The chill of the first nights softened and by mid-July I slept only on cotton sheets. The flannel sheets were put away until cold nights returned in late August. The days stretched out like cats lazing in the sun.

In that sagging, naked heat, Grace and I, Perry and the other children, never wilted. We melted into a caramel brown but remained startlingly white under our bathing suits.

Soon the sun started to take its toll on the land. The pasture behind the cottage singed but somehow the flowers on the roadside always stayed alive, turning their heads to the long summer sun. My mother was ever present but always gave us our freedom. If we were near the cottage, each morning before lunch she brought icy Kool-Aid, the very essence of summer, for us to drink. If we were away she went first to the back of the cottage and then to the dock and in each place she briskly rang her cowbell to call us for lunch.

On weekends my father arrived and absently busied himself. There was always something to saw, something to build or to repair, and whatever it was it was usually made from wood. In the shade of the grove of cedars by the dock he kept his sawhorses and there he would saw and saw, golden sawdust clinging to the sweaty hair on his brawny freckled arms and deep chest. At his feet sawdust collected in neat little piles as he cut deeper into sun-warmed woody pulp. To me, the sound of wood being sawed was the sound of summer. There was an almost biological rhythm to the sound, a digni-fied thrum, calming, contemplative, relaxing.

Our cottage had always been the last on the point, a dead end. Beyond was pasture where until early last summer Mrs Nichols' three milking cows grazed and drank from the water. Last July, one day when I returned to the cottage, Mrs Nichols was there having a cup of tea with my mother.

'Mrs Nichols has brought us some beautiful eggs,' Mum said.

'She tells me that Mr Everett wants his field back so we won't be seeing her cows any longer. She'll be grazing them elsewhere.'

I thought only children found Mr Everett, who owned the next farm on the paved road, scary but now I wondered whether adults did too.

When Mrs Nichols was leaving, my mother went to the door with her and holding Mrs Nichols' hand in both of hers she said, 'Everything will be all right,' and kissed her on the cheek. Mrs Nichols looked startled, then smiled and said, 'Thank you,' and left.

'Inside they're just like us,' Mum said to me. 'Christians are just so embarrassed to show their emotions.'

Then, at the end of that summer, builders arrived. They dug a foundation and now there was a big brick house, a year round house where the pasture had been, the first one that was built on the lake.

I was sad when that happened. The lake was for summer. The rest of the year it should be abandoned. It should have its life back, alone, but now people would live there year round. Besides, I liked being 'the end', the last family, with nothing beyond. No one ever drove or walked past our cottage. Now, looking south, it was no longer wild. I didn't see nature. I saw a perfectly manicured lawn. I didn't talk about that, not even with Grace. It was too painful.

But no one ever seemed to live in the big redbrick home. Someone came to cut the grass every week but the boat remained unused in the boathouse and seaweed gathered on the shore. From the time my father built our cottage I had waded in the water in front of where the new house now was, searching for crayfish, but one day a sign appeared on the lakefront, 'NO TRESPASSING'. When I saw that sign I stopped searching for crayfish and returned to the cottage, where my uncle was sitting in his lawn chair, contemplating the lake.

'There's a "no trespassing" sign next door,' I told him.

'Is that so? Let's have a look at it.'

Uncle Reub took off his black shoes, rolled up his city trousers just above his knees, and walked gingerly into the lake. I had never seen him do this before. Ever. It was the first time I had seen my uncle get wet.

We walked in the shallow water, only halfway up to my uncle's knees, until we reached the sign. Uncle stared at the sign. He said nothing then he put his hands on his hips and turned to me.

'There are lessons in life and one of them is that rules are made to be broken.'

He bent down and with his hands on his thighs he looked straight into my eyes. 'Always respect other people's property,' he said, 'but a sign like that is like slapping your neighbour's face.'

Uncle Reub gingerly walked through the water; his toes were podgy and pink and soft like little sausages. His shoulders went up with each step he took, until he reached the shoreline. He looked up at the empty big red house, stared at it for a little while then he reached for the sign and uprooted it from the ground.

'The fish will like this,' he said, putting the sign in the lake, and we carefully retraced our steps back to our cottage.

THE
VEGETABLE
PATCH

My father bought the land he built our cottage on from Mr Everett, and that wasn't easy. Mr Everett didn't like Catholics and he didn't like Jews. The Long Point Catholic and Jewish families knew this and had intermediaries buy their cottage land for them. When Dad told them he planned to buy land at the southern end of the point from Mr Everett, they warned him he might have trouble.

When the day came for Mr Everett to sign the legal transfer of his lakefront land he turned to my father, narrowed his gaze and said, 'Are you a Jew?' My father replied, 'I'm Scottish. I was born in Glasgow. That's why my children are named Robert and Bruce, and my dog Angus.'

'Are you a Catholic?' Mr Everett asked, and my father replied, 'I was born at 29 Ibrox Park Road. Do you think a

Catholic would live within spitting distance of Ranger's stadium?' Mr Everett's ancestors may have been English but even so he was aware of the rivalry between the Protestant Rangers fans and their Catholic Celtic Football Club rivals. My dad got the land without telling a lie.

On a May spring visit earlier this year, Dad created a vegetable patch for us. He'd wanted to go to the cottage on his own that weekend, but Mum had told him he should take me with him. We went for two days. It turned out very cold for that time of year – like March – and Dad put blankets on the windows at night to keep the cottage warm. He let the fire in the fireplace burn all day, adding logs even after I had gone to bed.

I was first up in the morning. I always was. Still am. I dressed quickly then lit a fire the way Dad had shown me, with dry twigs and scrunched balls of newspaper and old pine cones. I used the bellows to fan the kindling. It always sounded like popping corn on the stove as a fire lit up. Then I went out to the log pile and brought more logs in, not to burn just yet, but to dry first by the heat next to the fire.

I made breakfast for my father. That weekend he talked more.

'Good coffee,' he said. He never said that to my mother.

'Thanks for making breakfast.' I never heard him say such things to her.

After breakfast, Dad walked right round the cottage. He looked at the walls and the roof guttering, he got down on his knees and looked under the cottage where he stored his concrete breeze blocks and lumber. He inspected the dock and walked in and out of his boathouse. Finally he went into his tool house.

In summer, even on hot days, he spent a lot of time in there, surrounded by coils of ropes, inner tubes, fishing rods, boxes of tools – wooden ones, iron ones – rusty painted jacks, hoes, crowbars, winches, fishing line and tackle, heavy chains, old tyres, ceiling tiles, rolls of linoleum, boxes of pine cones for the fire, bags of charcoal, old wooden chairs, oil drums, oil cans, lawn mowers, shovels, forks and spades, tarpaulins, fishing nets, guttering, cardboard boxes filled with rusty iron nails, washers, nuts, bolts and screws, sawhorses, lead pipes, old trousers, vices, glass jars and bottles, gas tanks, bait traps, worm boxes with the dried remains of last year's moss and worms, kerosene lamps that were got out when the power failed, and it always did, with every single electrical storm. The tool house smelled of rust and rubber, tar and turpentine, varnish and shellac, fish scales and cedar. It was my dad's favourite place in the whole world. If you'd ask him, 'Do you want to spend a week at the Eden Roc Hotel on Miami Beach or a day in the tool house at Lake Chemong, everyone, even us children, knew what his truthful answer would be. Once I'd tried to tidy up the tool house and my father, with a stern voice he seldom used, told me to leave everything where it was. That's when I'd realised it was a sacred place, like the Ark that held the Torahs at synagogue or the steps up to the church at Sainte-Anne-de-Beaupré, and absolutely nothing, not a nail, not a rusty bolt, not an inner tube, not a piece of smelly rubber, should be disturbed in any way.

That cold weekend my father planted beds of red tulips along the back of the cottage outside the bedroom windows. He loved colour and never planted white flowers, although he collected Queen Anne's lace from the roadside to keep in vases on the kitchen table. He painted just about everything he got his hands on. After he'd painted the cottage white and the windows and doors cobalt blue he painted every single plant container in the garden, dozens of them, the same blue. He painted the porch floor blue and the veranda floor blue. He even painted the old enamel hand wringer washing machine blue, the one he'd put by the well, filled with earth and planted with climbing sweet peas.

Saturday was grey and horrible. Rain turned to sleet. My father decided it was too cold to leave the plants in the station wagon and brought them all inside where they huddled in the kitchen for warmth.

Whenever there was a job to do my father wanted to do it right away, regardless of whether that was sensible or not, so he told me to arrange the plants in groups that were all the same. Wearing a green Army poncho to keep out the freezing rain he went outside and, in the stinging sleet that was almost like snow, he cut a patch in the grass with his spade, about fifteen feet long and half as wide. That was the spade we later used at his funeral to throw earth on his coffin. He lifted the turf from that patch in strips and laid it in the muddy, water-filled tracks his car tyres had made on the road. Then he forked the black earth. Dad said it was the richest soil in the country, richer even than soil in the fruit belt around Niagara Falls. In April that soil drank the last of the melting snow. In May and June it was nourished by spring rains and in early summer by the morning dew. Before he built the cottage, when my father had drilled for water, he'd only had to bore twenty feet before he found the freshest, sweetest spring water. The soil even got nourishment from below. I watched my father out of my bedroom window, forking the soil, and thought he was steaming like a train engine.

After he finished preparing his vegetable patch, my father returned to the cottage, took off his poncho and sat on the rocker near the fire. Every line on his hands was blackened by the earth. His shiny, grey-flecked black hair and black, black moustache glistened with wet, and his freckles were lost in the red blush on his face.

'Did God make all the plants and flowers and seeds in the kitchen?' I asked.

'I got them from Canadian Tire,' he answered.

After lunch, my father went to the front of the cottage, facing the lake, and as he had done in the vegetable patch he removed the turf and turned over the soil on the gentle decline from the cottage door to the front lawn. He asked me to get the wheelbarrow and together we collected rocks from the shoreline, mostly from in front of our new neighbour in the big red brick house, and carried them back to the gentle slope where we placed them throughout the black soil.

'This will be a rock terrace,' he explained.

That evening he laid out all his plants and seed packets on the living-room floor, right where he counted the worms he caught on dewy summer nights, and moved them this way and that.

'Always have a plan, Bruce,' he said. 'A garden should look natural like it's not planned.'

My father called that 'studied carelessness'.

The next day's sunrise dazzled the soft earth in the vegetable patch and warmed me and my father.

'This land is so rich you don't need fertiliser. Anything grows here,' he explained to me.

He showed me how to use my forefinger to make a line of

holes in the earth, each one four inches apart, and when I had made one row he followed, enlarging them with his forefinger then placing carrot seeds in each one. In another row he planted cucumber seeds then several rows of potatoes he'd cut into quarters. He planted a row of dill to use for dill pickling in the summer.

After he finished, he collected the little seaweed there was from the shore and lay it in lines above the seeds.

'I thought they didn't need fertiliser?' I queried.

'That's for warmth,' Dad explained.

That may be, but in early summer my father would always bring wheelbarrows full of seaweed and cover the vegetable patch with it.

Dad went to his tool house and I visited the point, but all the cottages were still in hibernation. I walked up the track from Long Point to the county road. The crab apple, poplar, birch and maples were in leaf now. By the highway, lilacs on both sides were in flower and their scent was exhilarating to me. Along the roadside the first bursts of spring colour had appeared, yellow dandelions, buttercups and toadflax, rosy purple little fleabane and selfheal, early blue violets, white anemones and tinier white flowers of wild strawberries. Mr Everett's flax field was already a shimmering wave of light blue.

How can these flowers take care of themselves, I thought, but the ones my father was planting couldn't? Why are some plants dumber than others? Why do we have to make their decisions for them? I knew my father couldn't answer these questions so I didn't ask him.

When I returned from my walk down the point my father was planting a row of poplar saplings along the side of our property where Mrs Nichols' cows grazed last summer and where there was now the big brick house.

'By the end of summer we won't have to look at that house.'

For the very first time, I realised that although my dad didn't say much, he felt about the land just like I felt.

NOISE ON
THE POINT

I was in Grace's bunkhouse when I first heard the commotion. It sounded like a train was coming down the point. I didn't tell Grace but I felt an excitement and a dread all at the same time.

There was never any noise on the point during the week. There weren't many cars; the fathers took most of them back to work early on Monday mornings and Grace's mother seldom used hers. Besides, a car never made a noise like that, even if its muffler had holes in it. Milk and bread delivery men arrived each day: they were the best way to send written messages to cottagers further up the lake, but everyone knew the throaty sounds of their wagons. Motorboat engines were completely different. Grace and I were so familiar with boat sounds we could tell if a boat approaching had a Johnson or an Evinrude motor or was a Shepherd or Chris-Craft inboard. This was different. It was loud, whining and relentless.

Although the cottagers came from both Peterborough and Toronto, we were a tight-knit group. Organic. Self-assured. Everyone knew what the rules were, how to behave during the summer. I thought that if anyone was going to do something that made that much noise they'd surely tell their neighbours first.

The summer people employed local people to cater to our needs, to build our docks, remove our garbage, store our boats for the winter, install massive television aerials that I thought were big enough to communicate with aliens. We summer people fulfilled our dreams at our summer cottages. We escaped the heat and humidity of the city. We turned to a more natural way of life, simple and languid and still. We caught our own fish and grew our own tomatoes. We planted flowers and made our homes pretty and warm and cosy because cottage life was the reserve of women and children.

With the light painted walls in our cottage, my mother ensured that the sun always shone into our lives. Most of the other cottages were quite dim inside – their dark wooden walls were varnished, not painted. There were gingham tablecloths on the tables and crocheted doilies on the fabric-covered wooden sofas and chairs, all lit by the glow of lamps with milky glass shades. If there was one thing that united the interiors of all the other cottages of the summer people it was Quebec woodcarvings. Sometimes they were of moose or bears but more often they were of people, poor people, bent over, almost broken, all looking forlorn, wrinkled, with pursed hands and hanging clothes on their hunched bodies. They stood in each cottage, like lost souls forever separated from each other. I wondered whether they were there to remind the summer people how their grandparents lived.

Bunkhouses were for kids and visitors, bunk beds and a chair or two, but not much more. Grace and I were in her bunkhouse not doing much when we heard the commotion and went down the point to see what it was.

'Mary mother of God!' Grace exclaimed when we got to the track leading up to the county road. It looked like a tornado had run down its length, destroying everything in its path.

I was dumbstruck.

'Where did you learn to say that?' I said, staring into Grace's eyes but she had no time for me.

'Jesus, almighty Christ, what are you doing to my woods!' she thundered at the man driving the tractor, bulldozing the trees.

Above the roaring noise of the tractor's diesel engine there was a terrible splintering sound as another tree cracked and gave way to the mechanised onslaught. From where the tractor was, all the way up to the county road, what the day before had been a shaded green tunnel through overhanging branches of twenty-foot-high trees was now open to sunlight, littered with saplings and trees all with broken backs. At the top of the hill, the lilacs were ripped from the earth, motionless on the ground. Pushed to the sides were moss-covered boulders that had not budged a foot since the last ice age.

Grace was in a rage, trembling with an anger and a frustration I had never seen before. I tried to soothe her.

'It'll be OK,' I said.

'Will it? Will it? He's killed my trees. Where are my snakes?'

All the girls were frightened of snakes but Grace wasn't. In the narrow shaded woods that lined the track up the hill she had once seen a ball of garter snakes plaited together so firmly it seemed to her they would never unravel. That was on a visit in the spring and now in the summer she returned every single day. At first she caught snakes and took them back to her bunkhouse to play with, then back to the woods to release. Then she decided that wasn't fair to them – to get caught – so now she visited just to watch them. Only two days before she had seen a tiny garter snake and decided one of the bigger ones had just had babies.

Relentlessly the tractor continued to push its way through the trees. With her lips pursed and her hands on her hips Grace marched to the front of the machine and the driver brought it to an abrupt halt.

'You trying to kill yourself?'

It was Mr Everett, the farmer. I had heard my parents talk recently about Mr Everett. They called him a bigot and I'd asked Uncle Reub what that meant.

'You're killing my trees!' Grace shouted at him. 'I'm getting my father – right now.'

'Go on then, just keep out of my way. Your father's paying me to do this.'

'You're a bloody liar,' Grace replied.

I remained quiet. I was frightened of Mr Everett and I thought Grace was getting herself into trouble but I didn't say so.

'Your father's paid me to widen your damn road. Now stay away,' the farmer shouted at Grace and he returned to his tractor.

'Scram!' he barked at us. He waved his arms at us. 'Scram!'

'We'd better go,' I implored Grace, and taking her arm I led her off the track onto the road behind our cottages. We sat down and for the first time ever I saw tears in Grace's eyes.

'It's not fair!' she said, picking up gravel and throwing it hard against the ground. 'Why do they have to change things?'

'They just do,' I answered.

Holding her hand, kicking the gravel with my bare feet, we walked back down the road to Grace's cottage. The horrible noise continued all morning and Grace never saw snakes by that road ever again.

FISHING FOR
MUSKIES

Weekends were extra special. They didn't just feel different, they looked different too. During the week the gravelled road behind the cottages was almost empty. On weekends there was a car behind every cottage sometimes two, even more – Monarchs, Pontiacs, Oldsmobiles and Mr Fitzpatrick's fiery red Cadillac convertible that he was always washing and polishing. The mothers looked different too, especially mine. During the week they dressed any old how. Grace's mother did her gardening or hung out her laundry or just lay there on her lawn chair browning herself in the sun in her bra and shorts. During the week my mum only mentioned our dad when we misbehaved. 'If you do that again you'll have to answer to your father,' she'd shout at us. On weekends the mothers looked prettier. Anyways, that's what I thought. Each Friday morning my mother washed her hair. Sometimes in the bath or, if it was a sunny, hot day, in the lake where she washed ours. She spent the rest of the morning in curlers then after lunch she put on her makeup and did her hair. On Fridays she changed the bed linen and in the afternoon ironed the dress she put on for my dad's arrival. Sometimes he left work early and got to the cottage by late afternoon. He usually arrived later at night and I saw him the next morning.

One weekend, all the fathers gathered at Grace's cottage. They were going on a whole day fishing trip, up past Kelly's Island, past Mud Lake Reserve into Lake Buckhorn where Grace's father said he'd heard bass were biting. I knew I shouldn't even ask if I could go with them. I knew why they'd say no. This was a man's trip and I wasn't yet a man. I wondered whether they'd ever think I was. They didn't invite Uncle Reub either, and I wondered whether they thought he too wasn't a man.

Friday had been stormy but on Saturday morning the lake was shimmering and soft with just a little chop as dawn broke. You could tell it would stay like that all day. It was on tranquil days like that, after turbulent weather, that big fish bit. That's what grown-ups told me.

My father always set bait traps on Friday night when he got to the cottage but in case he didn't catch large-enough minnows he had stopped at a large house with a wraparound veranda just outside Peterborough on the road to Bridgenorth, a house with a hand-painted sign 'BAIT' on its front lawn, and had bought a bucket of five-inch-long sucker minnows.

I wanted to catch a muskie too and my father had let me take three of those minnows. I put them in a bucket of water in the shade under the cedars and at breakfast asked my uncle if he'd like to go muskie fishing with me.

Mum made a packed lunch for us, a peanut butter and banana sandwich for me, a tinned salmon and tomato sand-wich for her older brother and a thermos of Kool-Aid for us both. She got out a black umbrella.

'Reub, take this to keep the sun off your head.'

'Let's go,' I demanded.

By the time we were ready to go, the fathers were long gone.

I put my life jacket on, put the bucket in the rowboat, helped my uncle get in and rowed out onto the lake towards Kelly's Island, to exactly where I knew there were muskies because I'd seen them there when I flew over the lake in one of my flying dreams.

That night, in bed, I had listened to the mournful wail of two loons. Of course I knew they were loons. All the summer people knew the sound they made at night. To me that was the very best sound of summer on the lake – that pair calling each other, the first plaintively asking, 'Where aaaaaare you?' and its mate, out in the dark calling back, 'I'm over heeeere.' Even though I knew it was loons making those calls I still thought no animal could possibly produce such a movingly beautiful sound. Maybe it's really lost Indian spirits calling each other, I thought.

Only a few hundred yards off shore, my uncle whispered, 'Stop. Over your shoulder. Loons.'

As I turned around, first one dived then the other.

'Let's wait,' Uncle said.

It was two or three minutes before both birds reappeared, one almost a hundred yards away, the other close to the silent rowboat. It sat low in the water but it was so close I could see its piggy little orange eyes and the pure white feathers on its chest.

'Those two are mates. It doesn't matter what happens, they will always be there for each other, forever,' Uncle explained.

'Then what happens when one of them dies?' I asked. I didn't like that word 'forever'. My mother was always saying, 'Nothing is forever.'

'Do you mean does it go to heaven?' my uncle asked.

'No, I mean if one dies. Then they can't be together forever,' I said, proud that I was being so logical.

'You're right, everything dies eventually. What I mean is when one loon dies, the survivor remains faithful to it forever. It never goes off with another mate. It never breeds again. It lives out its life alone. Animals are honest and pure.'

'Does that mean they're better than we are? When Mrs Fitzpatrick died, Mr Fitzpatrick got married again and had more children.'

My uncle avoided a reply.

Instead I asked, 'Should I kill the minnow before I put it on the hook? I don't like putting a hook through its face if it's still alive.'

'Are we at the fishing hole?' he responded.

'Not yet,' and I resumed rowing for a while longer until we were close to Kelly's Island, where I stopped and gently lowered an anchor I had brought along into the water.

Uncle Reub looked into the minnow pail, at the minnows, all staying perfectly still because they had no place to hide and now he answered my question.

'How do you think you'd feel if someone big and powerful put a hook through your mouth and nose?' Before I could answer he continued. 'I bet you'd wriggle and try to escape.'

'But I want to catch a muskie before Dad does and he says muskie lures don't work and you need big minnows.'

'Do you want a muskie so bad you'd be cruel to the minnow?' my uncle continued.

'It's the same as catching a muskie. They get caught on hooks but it doesn't hurt them. Anyways, minnows wriggle and squirm because they're out of water,' I replied.

My uncle smiled. 'But what if, just what if it really does

hurt, that you hurt the minnow or hurt the muskie when you hook them? Are you happy to do that?'

'Dad's not cruel and he hooks his minnows through their mouths,' I replied.

My uncle said nothing. He looked out over the lake, back to the Long Point shoreline with its cottages nestled in the trees. He was silent for over a minute then he said, 'Bruce, fish suffer just as much as people do, they just can't tell you about their suffering.'

I didn't know what to say. I wished I hadn't brought my uncle with me in the first place but rather than say that, I grabbed a minnow from the bucket, held it tight in one hand, pushed the hook through its face and dropped it over the side of the boat. I said nothing. Nor did my uncle. The minnow stayed for a few seconds then ever so slowly it started to swim away and as it did I let out my line.

The day had become hotter. I saw sweat on my uncle's head and handed the umbrella to him. 'Use this,' I said, with a command in my voice and my uncle did.

There we sat for a while, together but separate, until Uncle Reub said, 'Brucie, when I was a medical student I learned that as we develop in our mothers' wombs we evolve through all the stages that ever existed in all of evolution. It's hard to believe but when you were developing in your mother's tummy, before you developed lungs, you had gills, just like a fish. The nerves you have, the ones you feel pain through, fish have them too. Everything we have had its beginnings in animals more primitive than we are. Pain is there to protect us, or fish, otherwise we'd always be damaging ourselves and we wouldn't know it. It has to hurt the fish when something sharp is pushed into its body. It's just common medical sense that when that hook gets into it, it hurts. Didn't Angus feel pain when the porcupine shot its quills into him?'

I didn't want to hear that.

'How do you know?' I spat out.

'Bruce, you're a sensible young man. Tell me, what do you think? Do you really think that a fish won't feel it when you put a hook through its face, or that the crayfish you use won't feel anything either?'

My shoulders dropped but I said nothing. I'd thought about that before, when the bigger boys at the fort stuck pine needles in frogs' eyes or hung up snakes and left them to die. I wanted to say something to them but worried they'd think I was a sissy. I'd thought I might be hurting minnows and crayfish too when I put them on hooks but I didn't want to say so. I didn't even want to think about that because I loved fishing. It was one of my most favourite things to do, so all I could say was, 'I don't want to go fishing today.'

'Why don't we stay out here and have our sandwiches and look for the loons,' Uncle Reub suggested.

'I want to go home,' I replied and I picked up the oars turned the boat around and went back to the cottage.

That evening the fathers returned from their fishing trip to Buckhorn, reddened by the sun and the bottle of rye they took with them. I heard that not a single father had caught a single fish. That made me feel a bit better.

FISHING
FOR BASS

I didn't go fishing for almost two weeks after that but one morning, while Mum was getting breakfast ready, I wandered down to the end of the dock, looked into the still lake and saw a fat, green bass amongst the usual sunfish and perch. I couldn't help myself and felt a thrill and excitement all over. It didn't matter if a fish felt pain. I had to catch that bass. Then Mum called me for breakfast.

There were rules at the cottage, rules set down by my mother. She set the table but my brother and I always had to clean up afterwards. Our father and Uncle Reub were never asked to do anything, and never offered, although when he was there Dad barbecued every evening meal: thick, fat steaks, hamburgers and hot dogs, and also any big fish he caught. That week was my turn to clear the table and dry the dishes while Rob washed them, and by the time we were finished Uncle Reub was sitting on his lawn chair with his handkerchief on his head looking out at the lake.

It was another hot day with a sapphire sky. On days like that I imagined I was a lizard, basking on a rock, soaking up energy from the sun, but today I had a mission, to catch that bass.

I went to the icebox and got some worms I'd collected with my father two nights before. I was good at catching them, better than Robert who always gave up after a few minutes.

'The easiest to catch are the ones that are stuck together,' Dad had explained, and while I worked the dew-covered grass at the front of the cottage, Dad did the same at the back, each armed with a flashlight with a white handkerchief wrapped over the beam to dull its brightness. We brought our catch back to the living room, dumped them all on newspaper, counted them, discarded the ones we had accidentally torn, packed twelve at a time in moss-filled cardboard boxes and stacked the cartons in the ice box between the milk and watermelon.

'Why are there worms? What do worms do?' I once asked my uncle.

'All the soil in your garden has passed through those worms. That's what they do for a living. Pass earth through and make it more nutritious for grass to grow in, or your dad's tomatoes.'

I returned to the dock. The sunfish and perch were there, as they always were, but the bass was nowhere to be seen. If I cast out only a little ways those small fish would swim out to his bait and that's all I'd catch. I enjoyed catching pan fish, especially sunfish that put up the best fight. I felt responsible and grown up when my mother told me to go catch fish because she wanted to make fish soup. But right now I didn't want to catch small fry, I was after that big green bass, so I cast my bait as far as I could then gently reeled it in, pulling the bait faster over weeds or through the shallows where the sunfish and perch were visible. I did this again and again casting over arm from the dock with no luck, not even a nibble, but then, on one of those casts, I let the line slacken before I should have and instead of arcing over my head, the worm-baited fishing hook snagged in my bare back.

I knew exactly what I had done and felt embarrassed and foolish. If the hook had been somewhere else on my body I could reach I'd try to get it out myself before asking an adult for help, but I knew I couldn't so, carrying my fishing rod over my shoulder, I went inside and told my mother what happened.

Mum tried to be calm but from her voice I knew she was very upset. Briskly she took me by my arm back outside to her brother. Uncle Reub examined how the hook had entered my skin. It didn't actually hurt me when he moved the hook. It just felt tight – like I was attached to something rather than something was attached to me.

'Kid, get me some Mercurochrome,' he told his younger sister and my mother went off to get it from the medicine cabinet.

He pinched my browned skin hard between his thumb and forefinger.

'Everyone make mistakes,' he said, 'when we're young. When we're not young. Take a deep breath then hold it until I tell you to breathe again.'

I held my breath, like I did under water, felt my uncle tugging on my skin, then the tugging stopped.

'You're free,' he said, as his sister returned. He painted where the hook had penetrated my back with the dark red dye from the tiny bottle. 'At the Mayo we called this "monkey blood",' he said, looking up at his sister as he handed her back the small brown bottle. Without saying a word she took it back inside.

Uncle Reub took me by the hand and turned me around so we now faced each other.

'Brucie, sometimes we don't recognise our mistakes until it's too late. Sometimes we're too tired to try to not make the same mistake. Sometimes we forget we've made mistakes. Sometimes we forget we've forgotten.'

I frowned. I didn't understand why my uncle was saying such things. He continued. 'What are you fishing for?'

'Bass,' I answered.

'Fish bite best when you swing your line out from the side, like a baseball bat,' he suggested.

THE BONFIRE

S ometimes I was allowed to stay up extra late, until long after dark, and in early summer it didn't get really dark until long after I usually went to bed.

Perry and Steve from Cedar Bay were staying. Their parents had gone to Quebec City for a week. It rained that afternoon, the kind of rain that came and went faster than my uncle's moods. Mum entertained us all by reading another chapter of a Hardy Boys book she read to us on rainy days, then gathered all of us around the dining room table for a card game of five-handed solitaire.

'Reub, come and join us,' she told her brother. 'This takes concentration,' she added, as my uncle became the sixth player, sitting beside his sister who beat him every time they had the same card and needed to get it first on the right pile in the middle of the table. I could see he wasn't giving in. He really wanted to beat her but her reflexes were faster than his.

We played several games, then Mum told us to clean up the dining room and living room while she prepared dinner. 'Perry and Steven, you too. When you're in my cottage you know you follow my rules. Your mother told me you love meatloaf so that's what we're having, with fresh mashed potatoes from Mrs Nichols' farm. Reub, make sure they know where everything goes.'

Everyone talked right through supper. That's what we did, with Mum starting the talking by telling us about mischief other cottagers had got up to or by asking one of us what we planned to do tomorrow. As he usually did inside the cottage, Angus lay under the dining-room table.

The rain had stopped well before suppertime and after we cleared the table and washed and dried the dishes, as a treat for us Mum made a bonfire in the stone fireplace near the shore and told us we could roast marshmallows in it. She started with dried twigs from beneath the tree house and pine cones Dad had collected in the woods and kept in the tool house. On top of these she placed offcuts of lumber Dad bought from Mr Blewett. She added dried birch bark we had peeled from trees, also stored in the tool house, and scrunched and twisted newspaper. On top of it all she added fresh pine logs, oozing sap. Those pine logs sizzled like steaks on the barbecue and burned for a very long time.

That night, with no moon but under a sky dusted with stars, we turned out all the lights in the cottage and then there was only one electric light in the whole world and it was on the porch of the farmhouse on the hill, a mile away across the lake. Us boys, Rob and Angus and me, Perry and Steve with Uncle Reub and Mum, all sat on lawn chairs around the fire and said nothing. We simply stared at the dancing flames. Myriad thoughts raced through my mind. At one point I heard thunder in the distance and told everyone a storm was coming. 'That's not thunder,' Uncle replied. 'It's dynamite. It sounds like it's coming from up the lake, probably in the water.'

To me, nights like that around the fire were perfect, the stillness of the lake, the warm feeling of the bonfire on my cheeks, the jungle sound of crickets all around, the low voice of a single frog croaking in the reeds under the dock. And then my mother said, 'Time for bed.'

None of us wanted to leave.

'Right now,' Mum said, with a sternness we knew and respected.

'Kid, I'll tell them a story first. It will be short. Not one of my interminable ones,' Uncle Reub said, and in his soft soothing voice, staring into the fire, he began.

'Boys, those frogs you have around your fort reminded me of this story. Once upon a time there was a beautiful pale queen. She was so beautiful there weren't words you could find to describe her so I won't even try. You had to see this woman to see just how beautiful she was. Her voice was as soft as a cloud and, when she walked, the earth sang it was so happy to have her on it. I once saw her and after that I couldn't do anything but think of her – nothing else.

'This beautiful pale queen visited children but only at night, when they were asleep in their beds. Children who she visited in their sleep always woke up the following day feeling fantastic – that life was wonderful, that life was really worth living, although they never knew exactly what it was that made them feel that way. It's just what happened.

'But, boys, if you woke up from your sleep, and looked at the beautiful queen, there was nothing she could do about it, she turned instantly into a frog, like the one we're listening to in the reeds or the ones at your fort in the woods. And forever more you could never tell her from any of the other frogs on the shore.

'Boys, that's why, although a frog is ugly and they feel clammy and you may not think a frog means much, when you pick one up, you should be kind to it. You should respect it. Because every single night, when the pale queen visits children, one child or another always wakes up and looks at her. And every morning that means that one more frog is really an indescribably beautiful woman caught forever in the body of a frog.'

A CANOE
PADDLE

When I wanted to be alone with my thoughts I would pick up Angus and take him to the canoe where we both did nothing. Just sit.

My father had found Angus sitting beside the highway one evening two years before. Angus was a thoughtful dog. That's what I felt. At night he slept in a wicker basket in my clothes cupboard and stayed there until I got up for breakfast. When he first arrived he never tried to get on my bed but now that was his favourite place to sleep, on cold nights under the covers. When he was inside the cottage he was content to spend his days in his basket. When he was outdoors he had two different personalities. On still, sultry days when the sun sizzled and Angus's back felt as hot as the shellacked bow of the motorboat, he was a calm dog. He would walk into the lake, sit, and for ages look down towards the bridge. On days like that he always kept his feelings deep in his own heart.

Then there were times when he behaved like an animal. I could tell he was looking for mischief by the way he walked out of the cottage, his ears perked, his tail high. That's when he'd go off to our neighbours or into the woods and come back covered in burrs or smelling of skunk. When he was sprayed by a skunk my mother would open a large can of tomato juice and hand it to me saying, 'He's your dog. Take him down to the lake and wash him with this.' There was one occasion when I was in the boat and he followed me into the lake. Grace was rowing over to her cottage. I was sitting on the stern of the rowboat with my feet dangling in the lake when I saw Angus swimming after us.

'Stupid dog!' Grace exclaimed. 'What if I was rowing to Kelly's Island?'

After Grace stopped rowing and Angus reached the boat, I pulled him in by his collar. He shook his curly hair getting Grace all wet and then he just sat and looked over the side at the far shore.

'I want to go home,' I told Grace.

She didn't say anything except 'Stupid dog!' but she turned the rowboat around and rowed back to my dock.

Today I didn't feel like talking to anyone. I picked up Angus and carried him to the canoe where we both sat in our own worlds. Then Uncle came over.

'You know, Angus is a grown-up. Does that mean the two of you are going for a paddle?' he asked.

'No he's not and no we're not,' I answered.

'There's a farm auction near Lakefield. Your father asked me to ask you if you want to go.'

I didn't answer. I lifted Angus and put him on the dock where the dog stayed. Then I got out of the boat.

'Angus! Come!' Uncle exclaimed and he got down low and spread his arms wide. The dog's tail lifted and wagged and he walked over to my uncle.

'See that smile? He's happy your family has given him a safe place to live.'

Sometimes I liked being with Angus and sometimes I liked being with my uncle. Right now I wanted to be alone with my dog but I knew I had to go with my parents. I didn't say anything. I picked up my dog and carried him into the cottage then went to the car and stayed by it until my parents and my uncle joined us and we drove to the auction.

The sale was on a concession road that was never oiled. Looking out the back window of the car I watched the rolling clouds of dust obliterate everything in sight. Evil spirits were chasing me. The spirits continued down the road when my father turned our car up the track to the farmhouse.

The field by the barn was filled with dusty pick-up trucks and I knew that our car was the only one that brought summer people there. There were plenty of strangers, all men, outside the barn looking at farm equipment – a red front-end loader Massey Ferguson tractor, a three-furrow plough, a green International Harvester pick-up truck with a snow plough attached, manure spreaders, water troughs, hay feeders, pig-farrowing crates, oat rollers, a post hole auger, hay, straw.

My family walked over to the front lawn of the farmhouse and moved up and down, back and forth, inspecting everything laid out with numbers on it. There were snowshoes, hockey sticks, meat saws, cast-iron radiators, kerosene lamps, tractor chains, milk cans, fishing nets. I thought the farmer must have a tool house even bigger than my father's.

'Morris, we could use those wooden wheels for the sweet peas to climb on.'

'Good,' Dad absently replied, looking at a barrel smoker, opening and closing it, seeing how it worked.

'Do you think he heard me?' Mum asked me.

'Let's have a look in the barn,' Uncle suggested, and we walked over to it. Dad stayed to inspect tools and machinery on the lawn.

Outside the barn there were big pigs, snorting and wallowing in rich, black mud.

'Darling, you see why we don't eat pork?' Mum asked.

'They're just having fun,' I answered.

'Good clean dirt never hurt anyone,' Uncle added, to no one in particular.

Inside the barn I could hear cows mooing but, at first, in the darkness and with so many big men in front, I could not see them.

My mother took me by my hand and we walked through the crowd until we were by a stall filled with cows.

'What type of cows are they?' I asked my mother.

'I don't know.' She paused for a while. 'Don't they have the most beautiful eyes? Ask your uncle.'

'They're shorthorns, Brucie,' Uncle said. 'When you see black and white cattle they produce milk. Black ones are for meat but these brown and white do both. There must be a milking parlour somewhere here because of those milk churns outside, but these look like they're for meat.'

I peered through the wooden slats, wondering how my uncle, who knew everything, knew these animals would make steaks for the barbecue, not milkshakes for Dairy Queen.

'They'll auction the livestock and equipment first, so let's have our picnic now,' Mum said, and we returned to the car, except my father who continued to tinker with items on the front lawn.

Mum used the station wagon's tailgate to lay out smoked salmon sandwiches for the adults, tinned salmon for me because I didn't like smoked salmon, homemade almond cookies, Kool-Aid for me, and a thermos of hot tea for the grown-ups. As we sat on the tailgate and ate, the farmer's yellow dog cautiously approached.

'He's hoping we'll give him something,' Uncle said.

'Shoo. Go away,' my mother scolded.

Watching the dog slink off I said, 'If they're shorthorns, why don't they have short horns?'

'They do, Brucie,' Uncle replied. 'The farmer saws their horns off when they're young so they don't injure him with them. That dog probably enjoyed chewing on those horns.'

'Why would they want to injure the farmer?' I asked.

'It's not that they want to. Cows are big and clumsy and horns are sharp.'

'Did it hurt, cutting them off?' I asked.

'I'm sure it did,' my uncle replied, 'but they look fine now.'

'I think they're better the way God made them,' I said.

From our car we could hear the auctioneer asking for bids although we could not make out what he was saying. Uncle went back to the barn to watch and listen. I stayed with my mother who closed her eyes and turned her head to the sun. 'I bet Noah's Ark was like inside the barn,' I said to Mum.

'Yes it was, dear,' she answered.

By the middle of the afternoon the auctioneer had sold everything in the barn and moved to the veranda of the farmhouse. I could see the crowd was now much smaller and they were mostly talking to each other and not paying much attention to what the auctioneer was saying. My mother and father and uncle were. During the afternoon, Dad bought three canoe paddles, some chain, a set of old wood chisels and a box of rusty ten-inch spikes. When he failed to buy the barrel smoker he turned to me and said, 'I'll make one of those.' At the very end of the auction, when the auctioneer got to the contents of the cardboard boxes on the veranda, he bought two handmade quilts for twenty-five cents each.

'They're filthy,' Mum said.

'They're for the hot water tank,' he replied.

Most days there's an afternoon breeze on Lake Chemong but when we returned to the cottage it was as hot and humid as the farm was. Rob was still at Steve's. Angus had been in all day so Mum let him outside. Dad took his purchases to the tool house while my uncle and I carried the paddles down to the dock.

'Shall we see how they work?' Uncle asked.

'But you don't like canoes,' I answered.

'Angus will calm my nerves.'

He got down low, opened his arms wide and called, 'Angus!' and Angus scampered over to him.

He carried the dog to the dock, put him down, then gingerly stepped in and sat on the bow seat holding both gunwales with his hands. Once the canoe settled he turned to me and said, 'Pass Calm Dog to me.' Which I did. I knew what Uncle Reub was doing, giving Angus another name, the way Indians do. Uncle put the dog down by his feet.

'Now put your life jacket on,' Uncle told me.

'You should too,' I answered.

'I don't need one,' Uncle replied.

I put my life jacket on, handed a paddle to my uncle then got in the stern of the boat with the other two paddles. One was a flat-sided beaver tail, good for straightforward deep water canoeing. The other was an otter tail with more rounded sides, better for the short, quick strokes you make when paddling in the stern. They were made from solid maple. I wanted to try both.

'Untie your end,' I told my uncle, then I untied the stern rope, pushed the canoe away from the dock and paddling hard swung the canoe out into the lake.

'Don't do anything yet,' I told Uncle Reub, who balanced himself on the bow seat with Angus sitting at his feet.

Grace's father had shown me how to use a paddle, to keep my back straight, to use my whole body for power, not just my arms. To push at the top and pull at the middle, to bring the paddle back in a J shape to hold a straight line. I had watched Mr Muskratt paddle his canoe. That's who I wanted to be in a canoe.

'You can paddle now,' I told my uncle, then added, 'did you and Edgar go canoeing?'

'No. His people used nets. There are big fish in the Missouri River. Pike. Pickerel. That's what they netted. Sometimes they stunned fish with a stick of dynamite. Boom, and they all float up to the surface.'

'You're rocking the canoe. Don't lean over when you paddle,' I commanded.

Then something that sometimes happens on the lake happened. A surface wind arrived. It didn't make waves but like an invisible hand it pulled the canoe away from the shore and I decided it was best to go right back home. I tried to turn the canoe around but in the surface wind it was difficult to do.

'Paddle on the other side,' I told my uncle, but every time he put his paddle in the lake he leaned so much the canoe almost tipped over.

'Stop rocking the canoe!' I bellowed.

'It's harder than it looks,' Uncle answered.

'Angus would be better than you. Don't paddle. Just sit!' I screeched and Uncle Reub did so, once more holding both gunwales in his hands to control the rocking.

I paddled hard on one side, trying to turn the canoe towards home and that didn't work. Then I tried going backwards and turning my paddle in a J and that almost worked, but each time I had almost turned the canoe around, another gust of wind caught it and turned it back towards the far side of the lake.

'Uncle, get on your knees and crouch down. Low.'

That was where Angus was sitting so Uncle squashed Angus under the canoe's bow then kneeled down and lowered his body still holding the gunwales.

'That's better,' I said, and now as I stroked my paddle backwards in the water, the canoe did turn in the direction I wanted it to and paddling as hard as I could I headed the boat straight back to the dock.

When the canoe entered the protection of the bay, paddling got easier. 'You can get up now,' I told my uncle.

Angus moved out from under the bow, gave his body a shake and woofed. As soon as the boat was close enough to the dock he jumped onto it and ran back onto the lawn, woofing some more.

'Calm Dog didn't like being ballast,' Uncle said.

'You should have had a life jacket on,' I replied. There was anger in my voice.

I tied up the canoe and went in the cottage but didn't tell Mum how foolish I thought my uncle was.

WALKING TO BRIDGENORTH

'Are there snakes in heaven?' I asked my uncle. 'Because if there are there must be chokecherries too. Snakes eat chokecherries. If you do, you choke and you die.'

'Who told you that?' Uncle asked.

'I made it up but everybody knows that.'

Uncle Reub and I were friends again and were walking to Bridgenorth. I was allowed to cross the county road but never to walk alone along it all the way to Bridgenorth. Mum sometimes did, especially when Dad was there. She'd say, 'I need to get out,' take her blue pack of cigarettes, and walk all the way, but even so she said it was too dangerous for me to walk there. Few cars used the county road that paralleled the eastern shore of Lake Chemong, and anyways you could hear them half a mile away. As they drove by the drivers always waved an arm from the open window but she still wouldn't let me walk alone.

It was one of those hot and hazy and humid July days when it seems that the whole world has slowed down to an idle. Grace was away. I was bored, so I asked my uncle to go for a walk. I didn't tell him what my plans were because I knew Uncle Reub didn't like walking far.

We walked down the point, then up the now cleared and barren track to the county road, the only paved road in the whole township, split and broken by winter freezes, its potholes patched with black asphalt. The highways department oiled it once a month during the summer but only remnants of the last oiling were visible on the dirt shoulders. We walked past the small sand quarry where kingfishers lived, past the Nichols' farm, past a field of sunflowers, a new sight in that part of the countryside, then through wild flowers that had colonised the verges of the road, when I asked about snakes in heaven.

I was barefoot. I always was. Ahead of us the bleached road disappeared into a shimmering mirage garlanded by those summer flowers, lush bushes and trees. There was blue chicory four feet high, in a long procession as if it had been intentionally planted on both margins, and behind the chicory on the lake side a bank of tiger lilies grew in the drainage ditch. Past the tiger lilies was a thick bed of alfalfa and everywhere, milkweeds, already in flower, already home to hundreds of striped black and yellow and white caterpillars eating their leaves, immune to the poisons that protect milkweed from almost all other insects, starting their evolution into Monarch butterflies that in a few weeks would fill the air around the cottage.

We walked past colonies of goldenrod, taller than I, the yellow buds about to open, a sign that August was shortly upon them. Then black-eyed Susans. They annoyed me. I thought they were the most beautiful of all the wildflowers along the road but their stems were so tough I could never collect them.

Beyond the drainage ditch in the shade of the trees that lined the road were the chokecherries that had caught my eye.

'There. Look. Chokecherries. There might be snakes here,' I said, and we stopped for my uncle to see what snakes ate.

He looked at the chokecherries then cupped his small hands on both sides of his tiny chin.

'I see,' he said. 'That's what I call bittersweet nightshade and you're absolutely right, those berries are poisonous.' He bent down and picked a flower. 'You see these blue flowers with their backward-pointing petals around those yellow beaks? Those flowers turn into red berries, what you call chokecherries.'

For a while we just stood there on the side of the road doing nothing much, listening to the silence, and pretty soon we could hear the flies and insects talking to each other, first a few, then dozens. Listening harder I heard millions, filling the hot air with waves of energy.

'Why did God make so many insects?' I asked, and my uncle didn't immediately answer. He looked out, over the field to the lake, his brow furrowed.

'Why did he?' I asked again.

'I don't know why,' my uncle answered.

'When will you?'

'I need to sit down,' Uncle Reub said and we sat in the shade on two granite boulders. My uncle picked up a rough pebble of pink granite and white quartz. He spat on it and rubbed it and it was much prettier.

'If you cover it in corn oil it will be pretty all summer,' Uncle said then he continued.

'Your mother believes in a white-haired God who lives beyond the clouds. She believes that God made these flowers and all those insects and that he controls every single thing that happens in this world. She believes that each year, on the Day of Atonement, he decides who will live and who will die. Not just which people will live or die but which insect will buzz with life and what flowers will survive and blossom.'

'Don't you believe that too?' I asked.

'I don't yet know,' my uncle replied.

I didn't like that answer. I'd heard my uncle say things like that before.

'Well, if you don't yet know, what do you believe in right now?' I demanded, my voice sterner than I wanted it to be.

My uncle paused once more, then turned to me and with mischief in his eyes said, 'I believe in fine-looking women. I have seen women whose smiles shine with such light I've been unable to move. I've seen women who are so stunningly beautiful I thought I'd faint. When I see women like that I can believe in God.'

'Well, I believe in God,' I said. 'Sometimes I dream I'm with God in heaven on the clouds and I can fall from the sky but I'm not scared because I'm with God. I like that feeling.'

'When do you have that dream?' Uncle asked.

'If I concentrate on having it, it doesn't happen. I have to wait for it to happen. Then I fall and glide through the air as long as I want wherever I want and see the whole lake and the cottages. I see where the big fish are in the lake and where to go swimming. I see the weeds and know I shouldn't go swimming there. I even see boats that have sunk but there are never any dead people in them.'

'Brucie, when I was a boy I kept a diary. Every day, either in the morning or at night I wrote down my thoughts, not what I did or where I went but what I was thinking about. What you think about is very interesting. Have you ever thought about writing it down?'

I thought that I loved the heat but my uncle didn't. As I thought that thought, I watched Uncle Reub take his large cotton handkerchief from his back pocket, tie knots in all corners and lay it on his head.

'Edgar Ten Fingers told me what he believes in. He says that anything that has a birth – a fly, a flower, a snake, you and me – must also have a death. Your spirit doesn't have a birth so your spirit never dies. He says that the rock is the grandfather of all things, the earth is the grandmother of all things and the sun gives motion and life to all things. He says the warmth of the sun entered the bosom of grandmother earth and she produced all the insects and animals and flowers and trees. I like how he thinks.'

'What happens after you die then?' I asked and again my uncle was slow to answer.

'Your mother thinks you go to a place that's new and bright, where everyone understands each other, and everyone and everything that ever died before is waiting. Everything is open and ready to be explored. Everything is spacious and there aren't any mysteries. That's what she believes.'

'But, Uncle Reub, what do you believe?' I asked.

My uncle got up and turned away. He said nothing and I wondered if he didn't want to tell me what he believed in because I wasn't yet a grown-up. Then he turned back to me. He spoke quietly and seriously. 'It's more important for you to understand how your mother feels. To her you and Robert are the centre of the universe and that's the way it should be. She thinks in the end everything will be better.'

He paused once more, again looked towards the lake and the cottage and now without turning back to me, he continued.

'In my life I've wandered into a dark forest and your mother is like an angel helping me out of it. I believe in her. That's what I believe in, Bruce. In people like your mother.'

My uncle slowly turned back towards me and now he was smiling as if he had won the Irish Sweepstakes. A car passed and the driver as always waved, an acknowledgement that we inhabited that empty land together if only for the summer.

'Are you thirsty?' Uncle Reub asked.

I was. We got up and continued walking. Bridgenorth was still almost half an hour away.

It seemed to me that Mr Everett always herded his cattle along that road for no particular reason and there they were ahead of us, swaying their enormous bellies, swishing their dung-covered tails, covered in flies. All were heading in the same direction, but now Uncle Reub and I walked carefully, avoiding the fresh cowpats. The cows turned up the long track that separated Mr Everett's verandaed stone farmhouse from his big red barn, but one hung back by the road grazing on chicory, cow thistles and dandelions. It raised its head and gave a short snort as we walked past.

'Cows have the most beautiful eyes, don't you think?' Uncle asked and without waiting for an answer continued. 'Don't you think Grace's eyes are like a cow's eyes?'

I had never thought about it that way but without saying so I agreed.

In Bridgenorth we stopped at the bait store across from the gas station, the only place in the village where we could get lunch. We both had grilled cheese sandwiches. Uncle had a ginger ale to drink and I an Orange Crush. My uncle needed that food and drink. The day had become hotter and his feet in his city shoes were hurting. We started back towards the cottage, past the summer cabins at Holiday Haven, past the green corn fields, past pastures with the smell of sweet hay, past the milk churns that were now on the roadside outside Mr Everett's farm. I really wanted to go into his barn, to see him milking his cows but I was scared of him so I didn't mention it to my uncle.

Nearing the cottage, it seemed to me that the sunflowers had turned their heads. Before lunch they faced the road. Now in the afternoon, they were looking straight down the road, right at my uncle and me. By August everything else on that road from Bridgenorth turned brown and died but I already knew that those dead flowers were patient. They waited silently and with resignation in their roots until the next year when they would burst into life as they had earlier this year, like a living rainbow along the asphalt road.

'The sunflowers follow the sun. They really do,' Uncle said. I wasn't surprised that my uncle knew what I was thinking.

'But they don't have muscles. How do they?' I asked.

'No one yet knows,' my uncle replied, 'although one day someone will, then we'll all know. Edgar told me he knows. He told me that once upon a time there was a boy who fell in love with the sun. Each day he would sit in a field, just like this one by the lake and watch the sun take its journey across the sky, from this side of the lake at dawn to the other side of the lake at dusk. The Oglala Sioux named the boy Sun Gazer.

'Brucie, you know what happens, don't you, if you stare at the sun? First it damages the retinas in your eyes but if you keep staring at it, it destroys them and that's what happened to Sun Gazer. He gradually went blind.

'Even when he was blind, he still loved that sun so much he sat in that field and guided by the penetrating heat of its rays on his face he followed the sun on its daily arc through the sky, from east to west.

'But in late August, when the heat had gone at night and the air had a chill, he became depressed, and dejected, and lost interest in life. He became sad and weak, and one day his tribe found the boy collapsed in that field, facing the west. And as the sun disappeared over the hills across the lake the very last spark of life left Sun Gazer and he was no more.

'That night the Oglala Sioux buried him at that spot and when they returned the next day to visit the grave they saw that a tall graceful flower had sprung from the mound and that the head of that golden flower bent gently towards the ground.

'They all gathered together that day, and in memory of young Sun Gazer they stayed from dawn until dusk and as they sat and showed their respect to the young boy they saw that the head of the flower followed the sun across the sky.'

I felt tears well in my eyes but I didn't say anything. The road started its incline up to the Nichols farm, and as we silently passed the black-eyed Susans that I thought were so beautiful, Uncle took his Indian knife from his pocket and, one at a time, being very selective, he cut over thirty stems.

'We can give these to your mother,' he said, then added, 'why not give some to Grace?'

THE WRECK

On a blustery, sunny Sunday, near the end of July, Mr Muskratt came paddling down the lake straight to our dock. Not stopping anywhere. There were whitecaps on the lake. It was too rough for anything but the big boats. He never visited on Sundays so it was exciting to see him there – paddling into the waves, so low in his canoe he looked like a beaver. He docked his canoe and in his expressionless way asked me, 'Your father here?' which he was.

The two men spoke for a minute then my father went into the boathouse, started the motor and backed his boat out. They tied the bowline of the canoe to the stern of the boat and were about to leave when I asked, 'Can I come?' and unexpectedly it was Mr Muskratt who replied, 'Yep.'

I liked Mr Muskratt. He wasn't complicated. He was just who he was. Every Friday he paddled his canoe down the lake from the Reservation, stopping at each dock, waiting to see if anyone came out to buy his fish. He never called out 'Hello' or 'Fish for sale'. If no one noticed him he just paddled on to the next dock, then the next until finally he reached our dock. After that he'd turn around and paddle back up the lake to his home.

I was surprised one Thursday to see him at the Quaker Oats factory in Peterborough. I didn't know that Indians worked in town. Grace's mother took her daughters and Rob and me to the factory where there was a tour of the premises. We were told in advertisements that Quaker Oats were light and puffy because they were made by being shot from cannons, and sure enough, in the last room on the tour, there was a big black cannon in the middle of the empty room surrounded by messy piles of Quaker Oats. Mr Muskratt was in a Quaker Oats uniform sweeping the corridor outside that room. He briefly said 'Howdy' to us all then continued sweeping.

We motored out into the lake and even though we were going with the strong wind, not into it, and were gliding over the whitecaps, my father drove slowly so that his wash didn't capsize the canoe. I sat up front. I loved getting splashed as the boat broached the waves. Dad was at the back and Mr Muskratt sat on the cross seat nearest him, occasionally shouting something over the motor's noise but I couldn't hear what it was. As we approached Kelly's Island I could see that Mr Muskratt was instructing Dad to slow down and go to the left. As we passed the island Mr Muskratt stepped to the front of the boat, where I was, and pointing with his right arm said, 'There!' My father slowed to trolling speed and headed for the wooded shore Mr Muskratt had pointed to.

The lake bottom was steep but rocky around Kelly's Island and as we neared the shore my father cut the engine and raised the motor out of the water. Mr Muskratt got onto the bow deck and using one of the boat's paddles, silently guided them along the edge of the boughs of the trees that overhung the lake.

'There,' he said and I saw it before my father did, an abandoned wooden boat, wedged in a locked embrace with the trees and shore.

I understood right away why Mr Muskratt had come to my father for help. He was the strongest man on the lake. Even Mr Muskratt knew that, and he needed all the help he could get to move that boat off the shore.

'Are there dead people?' I asked.

'Nope. Lost boat,' replied Mr Muskratt.

There was no motor on the boat but I could see it was a much better boat than ours. It looked the same length, had the same maker's name, Peterborough, on the side at the back and the same brilliant red-painted bottom below the splash rails, but inside it was completely different. Our cedar boat had two rear side seats to drive from and two cross seats with no back rests. This boat was also made of cedar strip but the inside was made of darker mahogany and, as well as a bow deck, it had a rear deck that made it look like an inboard. There was a white plastic-and-chrome steering wheel up front, even a glove compartment, and I thought it wasn't fair that we couldn't keep it ourselves.

Without rolling up their trousers or taking off their shoes, Mr Muskratt and my father stepped over the sides of the boat into the water. They were on the lee side of the island so the water was calm and they tied the bow rope to an overhanging branch. With one man on each side of the beached boat's stern they rocked it side to side but it didn't budge. Not an inch. They reminded me of a dog team working together, not having to tell each other what to do, silently just doing. Both men disappeared amongst the whispering tree boughs then I heard my father's voice, 'Heave!' Then again, 'Heave!' and again, 'Heave!' and again, 'Heave!' and I saw the boat start to move out a little from where it was locked.

Mr Muskratt reappeared from the trees. He untied our boat from the tree branch and led it to the beached boat where he roped the two boats together and, with a powerful thrust, pushed me in my boat away from the shore.

'Start the boat. Keep it in neutral. When I shout "Go!", gun it.'

Mr Muskratt disappeared back into the trees.

I put the gear in neutral, pulled the starter coil and the motor roared to life. I strained to listen above the engine's noise and when I heard 'Go!', I threw the gear into forward and rotated the steering handle to full throttle. The engine screamed. The propeller dug into the water with such power it seemed to empty the lake behind the boat of water. The bow bucked up but the boat didn't move forward. I kept the throttle twisted as far as it could go. I knew what my father and Mr Muskratt were doing, using all their strength to unlock the boat from where it was wedged. It took almost a minute, a long time with the motor roaring, but eventually I saw the bow of my boat come down a little and as it did I saw the beached boat slowly emerge from the trees. Instantly I reduced the throttle and pulled the gear back to neutral. The men emerged and silently they each inspected their side of the boat's hull. It was intact. It was seaworthy. They floated the boat onto the lake and it looked just perfect, its cedar flawlessly varnished. There was six inches of water in the boat itself. That's what made it so heavy to dislodge from the shore. I wondered why they hadn't bailed it first.

Mr Muskratt signalled me to turn off the engine. The men talked quietly, then Dad got in our boat and Mr Muskratt, with the paddle from his canoe, got in the rescued boat and like a string of ducks, with the canoe the duckling straggler, we set off slowly in the direction of Mud Lake. As we approached, at a point that they had previously chosen, my father idled the engine, untied the line and threw it back towards Mr Muskratt who pulled it in. Dad gave a wave to Mr Muskratt – really just a hand up – and I watched as Mr Muskratt paddled his new boat, the wind helping him, back to his home.

'Why didn't you bail the boat first?' I asked, and Dad told me he'd forgotten to take a bailing can with him.

'Why didn't he ask his friends on the Reserve to help?' I asked Dad as we watched Mr Muskratt ever so slowly glide away.

'He'd have to share the boat with them.'

Dad started the motor, turned the boat and headed back to the cottage. I thought that rescued boat with its extra-long bow deck, its rear deck, its cockpit to sit in, its sensuous shape, was so much more beautiful than the boat I was in.

'So will we share it with him?' I asked.

My father smiled and said, 'It's for him. He needs it more than we do.'

THE FLOATING
BRIDGE

T he residents of Bridgenorth decided to have a party on the
fifth anniversary of the new causeway, replacing the old
floating bridge across the lake, which was broken up and sold
off to cottagers.

The year my father built our cottage, 1949, was the last year
that Bridgenorthers could claim title to 'the longest floating
bridge in the world'. 'Isn't it a shame,' everyone had said, but I
didn't think so. The floating bridge had frightened me, that flimsy
and fragile bridge. When my father drove over it I was sure our
car would go through the thin cedar rails, sink to the bottom of
Lake Chemong and we would all die. 'Scared?' my father would
ask. I knew my father liked giving me a scare but had no idea why.
He never took me alone on drives across the bridge. He filled the
car with other children from the point, Grace and I always in
front with him, Rob and the others on the back seat. Grace was
always quiet, her brown eyes intent. I always teared up from fear.

*

Lake Chemong is a finger lake, ten miles long, created by gla-
ciers at the end of the last ice age. Uncle Reub had told us
stories about how farmers from Britain had arrived a hundred
years ago, cleared the forests and settled the land. He told us
how, after the eastern shore had been cleared of its richest
forests, after fields were laid out on the blackest soil and rid of
their ice age crop of stones, after livestock and crops were successfully raised on that land, a floating bridge was built across
the lake to access the western side. Irish Catholic families
already lived there, he said. The Scottish and Irish Protestants
on the eastern shore, our shore, called them 'the Fenians' and
their village, Ennismore, 'The Cross'. Loggers from the
sawmill in Bridgenorth had already cleared that land of its
best trees but the soil was good and crops grew well. To get
their crops to market, the Catholic farmers had to haul their
wagons around the bottom of the lake doubling the distance
to town. A steamboat service across the lakes proved too
expensive and so, in 1869, a floating bridge opened. It meant
Ennismore farmers could drive their livestock straight across
the floating bridge to the Peterborough market, less than
seven miles away. Sometimes their cattle bolted through the
split cedar wooden rails into the lake, but cattle are good
swimmers and most would make it to one shore or the other.
Horses were more reliable. If you were in a horse-drawn
buggy Uncle said you were safe. Horses halted, even in the
most miserable sleet of November, when they reached a
section of open water where part of the bridge had broken
away in a storm.

Grace's father said that to build that bridge, half-ton rocks
had holes bored into them, then iron rods were placed in the

bore holes, then molten lead was poured in to secure the rods. Those were the bridge anchors. One end of a chain was attached to each iron rod and the other end to a massive white pine log. During winter, horses dragged these rocks and chains and logs out onto the ice, in a straight line from the bottom on Colborne Street on the Bridgenorth shore across to the far side of the lake.

When the ice melted the following spring those rocks sank, anchors that would keep the floating bridge in position, more or less, for over eighty years. The pine logs on those anchor chains provided staging for the cross timbers and plank sections of the bridge that was built out from near the sawmill on the Bridgenorth shore. A log boom twenty feet wide was anchored along the length of the floating bridge, to save it from ice damage during the winter but it didn't help much. There was always winter damage. Summer too. Steamers sometimes accidentally ran into it.

In that last year of the floating bridge's existence, when the local people called it 'the wandering bridge', my father drove us back and forth over the bridge for his own amusement. I was frightened most because looking out the front window of my father's car all I could see was water, not road, just lake water with parallel wooden rails on either side. Over time the squared cedar timbers under the surface planks had become so waterlogged the weight of a car sank the roadway below the lake's surface. At least on the bridge itself I could see the road's visible surface rising out of the water ahead of us. I could see the bridge was heading straight to the far shore. But the bridge wasn't wide enough for two cars. When we met an oncoming car Dad or the other driver had to move aside, into one of the five pull outs built alongside the floating bridge, and it was always my father, it seemed to me, who did. The car's weight meant the pull out was completely under water. All I could see was the ragged rail of the fence and the unending water up the lake and I was sure my father was intentionally driving us all off the bridge. When that happened the other children squealed with delight.

Back in 1949, Grace's father arranged that all the cottagers boat down to the opening of the new causeway in mid-summer. Our flotilla from Long Point had dropped their anchors a few hundred yards offshore from the lumber mill, watched the boat races, watched the Air Force Vulcan jets do barrel rolls over the new causeway, watched parachutists land in the water on both sides of the new structure. Grace's mother thought it would be fun to water ski under the new swing bridge, which she did although the bridge master got angry with her husband for letting her. There was a lot of shouting.

Today all the cottagers at our end of the point prepared picnics and in a gay, motley flotilla, motored slowly down the lake to the new causeway, just as we had five years earlier. There wasn't much happening except speeches so in convoy we passed under the swing bridge then headed for the western shore of the lake for a picnic.

It was hot and sunny but with a fresh breeze when we beached our five boats on a sandy strip of shore where cedars offered shade. Grace and I sat down on the shore to rummage through the seaweed and flotsam looking for treasures.

'My bubba says if you tell a lie you have to spit over your shoulder three times or God will be angry with you,' Grace whispered, out of nowhere.

'That's not true,' I replied. 'She says that because she has an accent. She's superstitious.'

123

'But what if it is true?' Grace asked. She found a red-and-white plastic float in the seaweed and was following the line it was attached to. 'I don't want God to be angry with me.'

I carefully tore apart the seaweed the line disappeared into. I too wondered whether we would find a good fishing lure at the end of the line, something we could use when we went fishing together.

'Only grown-ups lie,' I offered my friend in encouragement.

'Children sometimes too,' she replied then, stopping what she was doing, Grace turned her head over her shoulder to the lake and spat three times.

'What did you do that for?' I asked. I tried to sound unconcerned but felt uneasy. What dreadful lie had Grace told? Had she stolen something? Had she broken something precious and blamed her sister? Who had she lied to? Horrible thoughts raced through my mind and as they did she said, 'I lied to you. I pretended I wasn't worried about Angus when the porcupine shot him but I really was. I cried after.'

I wanted to look into Grace's eyes but she wouldn't let me. She just stared at the sand on the beach and drew parallel lines in it with her finger. She didn't seem comforted at all that she had confessed her lie to me but I felt curiously joyful, like a great weight had just lifted from my heart.

'Doesn't matter,' I said, and I continued to work my fingers through the seaweed, following the fishing line. Grace was silent as I pulled a lead weight attached to the fishing line out of the tangle of weeds.

'No lure,' I said. Grace only shrugged her shoulders.

We got up and walked to the water's edge where we washed sand and seaweed from our hands, then walked up the beach and through the cedar trees. I offered Grace my hand to help her up the steep bank. She took it and squeezed it tight, holding onto it until she could see where the mothers had laid out their picnic in the clover pasture. She quickly ran ahead of me and when she reached the picnic, turned and shouted, 'I'm the winner! I'm always the winner!'

THE MYSTERY

'The one reliable thing about Reg Muskratt is his unreliability.' That's what my mother said. She'd also say, 'He's a law unto himself,' or 'Don't set your clock by him.' Things like that. Sometimes Reg Muskratt appeared on the dot each Friday afternoon at 2 p.m., paddling his canoe down the lake from the Reserve, an oily tarpaulin covering the bass and pickerel he sold to the summer people. Sometimes he never visited at all. I figured he never thought a lot about the summer folk.

Mrs Muskratt was completely different. Every now and then, after it had rained for several days running and it seemed the sun would never shine again, Grace's mother piled all the children on the point into her car and drove us up to Mud Lake. It took much longer to get there by car than by boat. She had to follow the straight concession roads, up to the top of Lake Chemong to Selwyn, then west towards Buckhorn, then several miles down again, along a rutted and potholed dirt track she had to take very slow, to the end of the peninsula that separates Lake Chemong from Buckhorn Lake, to the Indian Reserve.

There were no telephones on the Reserve, electricity either. The houses were made of wood, white like our cottages, but smaller. Some had verandas but most didn't. Almost all had vegetable patches beside them. Mrs Muskratt never knew we were coming but was always smiles.

'Grace, what pretty barrettes,' she'd say, or, 'Bruce, don't you think you should have your moccasins on?' Her round cheeks were as shiny as her jet-black hair. Her neighbours the Whetungs had built log cabins on their land for summer tourists and took them fishing. It was Mrs Whetung's idea. That was no surprise, Grace's mother said. The women on the Reserve always seemed busier than the men. I thought the men never did much, not even talk. They sat on verandas or outside the store or by the gas pump and smoked hand-rolled cigarettes. Except for Mr Muskratt. He was never there when we visited and I knew he must be doing this or that, something or other. Like my father, Mr Muskratt seemed ill at ease, out of sorts, when he wasn't busy. I figured the two men were friends because neither of them ever had a single thought in their heads. On this visit I saw Mr Muskratt carrying boxes of fish to the Reservation's ice house.

'Done good fishing last night,' Mrs Muskratt said, when she saw me watching her husband.

On visits, Mrs Muskratt and Mrs Whetung always showed us how to make things ourselves, like tepees out of birch bark, fragrant dried sweetgrass and black cotton thread. They showed us how to make beaded bracelets. The women on the Reserve made these and more beautiful birch boxes, some small and round, others big enough you could use them to cover a box of

Kleenex, all decorated with dyed porcupine quills or coloured beads. The women told us they collected the quills in winter, cut birch bark in late spring and gathered and dried sweet-grass in early summer. We learned that one porcupine could provide thirty or forty thousand quills of all different lengths and thicknesses and that quilling took great patience as you had to pierce your design first then pull both ends of each quill through the birch bark. Small fingers were best doing this. The women sold their crafts to Woolworths in Peterborough where most of the summer people bought theirs, but Grace's mother always bought her beaded and quilled containers and boxes directly from Mrs Whetung and Mrs Muskratt. Once, driving back to the cottage, Grace's mother turned to Grace and said, 'Mrs Muskratt wears the pants in her family. She's running for Chief in the elections next week.' I worried that she meant that Mr Muskratt didn't have any pants to wear.

My father was the most successful fisherman on the point but even so I could see he was jealous of Reg Muskratt's fishing skills. When my dad took off a day's work and came to the cottage on a Thursday, he always followed Mr Muskratt with his binoculars the next day, hoping to see where he fished. But after emptying his canoe of his catch, Mr Muskratt always paddled straight back up the lake without stopping and my father always lost sight of him as he paddled past Kelly's Island.

Mr Muskratt's fish were always just right – like the pictures in my father's *Field & Stream* – fat and fresh, and although the lake teemed with fish and cottagers could catch their own, the sight of those bright green fish in Reg Muskratt's canoe was always picture perfect. My mother never passed up the chance of buying some. When Mr Muskratt visited the other cottagers he never got out of his canoe but if my father was there he did, tying his canoe to the dock, going off together to look at this and that. I burst with pride when that happened. 'Tonto and the Lone Ranger are making plans,' I'd tell Grace. We would go down and stare deep into his canoe. He didn't seem to much care for it, not the way the cottagers took care of theirs. The inside of his canoe was covered in dried dirt, and seaweed and fish scales. His handmade maple paddles were darkened with age, one blade repaired with black electrical tape. There were tarpaulins, nets and a flat granite rock bound by rope that he used as an anchor. Even from the dock we could smell the tar he used to repair leaks.

Sometimes, after Mr Muskratt and my father had finished whatever they were doing – taking apart the pump from the well, jacking up a corner of the bunkhouse and wedging rocks under it, he stayed and my mother prepared coffee and cake. The men didn't talk much other than about the job at hand but one day my father asked Mr Muskratt what I knew had been on his mind.

'Say, where do you go fishing?' he asked.

'The lake,' was the answer.

Dad went silent but I could see he wasn't happy with that answer.

'Use live bait?' he eventually asked.

'Nope,' Mr Muskratt replied.

'Lures?'

'Nope.'

Mr Muskratt finished his coffee, got up from the table, said, 'Next week?' My father nodded, and he left.

NOTHING
HAPPENS

As I finished drying the breakfast dishes and my mother put them back in the cupboard, she said, 'Go talk to your uncle.'

She tried to hide the tenseness in her voice but I knew when she was pretending everything was normal, and now she was pretending. Besides, before she made breakfast I'd heard her call him a fool and I knew that he wasn't. Children could be foolish but not adults, especially Uncle Reub. To me he was the cleverest adult, the most intelligent one, the one who knew almost everything and if he didn't know something he was honest and told you he didn't.

Uncle Reub was back in his chair on the lawn, looking down the placid water towards the bridge. Flies were bothering him because every now and then he waved his hand across his face.

'What should I talk about?' I asked.

'Just talk to him.'

I wanted to go to Cedar Bay to help Rob, Steve and Perry build a raft, but Rob had told me I wasn't invited.

'I'm going to take Angus for a walk,' I answered and my mother replied, 'After you do that talk to your uncle.'

I went in my bedroom where Angus was in the clothes cupboard in his basket, his big brown eyes wide open. I picked him up and looked into his eyes. They were the same colour as mine, dark chocolate, and for the first time in my life I wondered what it would be like to be a dog, to think like a dog. Did he think the way I did, wondering what he'd do today? Did he wonder why the clouds moved so fast? Did he know when Mum was moody and needed to be left alone or when she needed someone to just listen to her talk? I carried Angus outside and put him down, but instead of going for a walk we went over to my uncle.

'Mum says I should talk to you,' I said.

'Did she say what you should talk about?' Uncle asked.

'No, just talk to you.'

We were both silent. Angus wandered down to the shoreline where he found a dead sunfish, brought it back to the grass then carefully and purposefully rolled on it.

'Are you hungry?' I asked.

Uncle sat up straighter, turned to me and I noticed, also for the first time, that my uncle's eyes were as brown as Angus's and mine. 'We all look the same,' I thought. 'If our eyes look the same do we all think the same?'

'Your mother brought me a bologni sandwich.'

He paused then continued, 'Brucie, that's thoughtful of you to ask.'

They were silent once more.

'Nothing to do today?' Uncle asked.

'It's boring,' I replied.

'Have a look at my watch,' Uncle suggested.

I loved Uncle's watch. The numbers were large. In daylight the numbers and hands looked light green but at night they glowed in the dark.

'Watch the second hand.'

I did.

'Keep watching the watch.'

I did.

'Brucie, did you notice that time slows down when you watch it?'

It did take an awful long time for the second hand to go all the way around the dial but I said nothing until Uncle broke the silence once more.

'Do you know that my watch and the sandwich your mother gave me and the moon are all related?'

'How?' I asked.

'Brucie, science teaches you about relationships. Hundreds of years ago a man discovered a lump of rock that glowed in the dark. It was on a mountain outside Bologna in Italy. He was a religious Christian so he believed in the devil and called the rock the devil's stone. The devil is also called Lucifer so he actually called it "luciferous" stone.'

'Why is the devil called Lucifer?' I asked.

'I don't know. Christians believe there is a devil. They call him Satan or Lucifer.'

I looked straight into my uncle's brown eyes.

'Do you believe in the devil?' I asked and Uncle grinned.

'Yes. There's a bit of the devil in all of us,' he answered, 'but we were talking about bologni sandwiches and my watch. Because the moon glowed at night people thought that it must be made out of the same type of rock, luciferous stone, but Galileo knew that the moon glowed because it was reflecting light from the sun and that the lump of rock from near Bologna was a natural mineral called barium sulphide. My watch glows in the dark because it's made from barium sulphide.'

'Who's Galileo?' I asked.

'He was also a good Christian but a great scientist, perhaps the greatest. He knew the church was wrong about the stars and creation and he said so. You can be religious, Bruce, but that doesn't mean you must believe everything your religion tells you is true.'

I stared at a multitude of sky-blue damselflies hovering over the drying seaweed on the shoreline. Uncle watched me stare.

'What does religion say about why dogs roll on dead fish?' I asked.

'Let's go for a walk,' Uncle replied. 'I'd better get out of my pyjamas or your mother will get angry with me.'

As he got to the cottage door I called to him, 'What about your sandwich?'

'I'll finish it later,' Uncle replied. He went through the screen door but was back outside in an instant.

'You mean what's the relationship between my watch and my sandwich?' he asked and I nodded.

'It's a feeble one. That first glowing rock my watch is made from was found near Bologna in Italy where bologni comes from. If bologni is made from pork it's called bologna, like the town, but when it's made from turkey like your mother buys it's bologni. Everything I say is baloney but it's good to talk baloney.' Uncle smiled and disappeared into the cottage.

THE VISITOR

My father's grandfather was a blacksmith. I don't know my grandfather's occupation. All I know about my father's father is that he abandoned his family and moved to Chicago. My father fell into his own occupation accidentally. When his family lived in Ottawa, his oldest brother, Barney, fell in love with Evelyn Byng, the wife of Lord Byng, the governor general of Canada. Evelyn Byng loved flowers and he plied her with them, but buying daily from the local florist proved expensive. For access to flower wholesalers, Barney became a florist and my dad helped out in the flower shop. Evelyn Byng also loved hockey and donated what became the Lady Byng Memorial Trophy to the National Hockey League, given yearly to the most sportsmanlike and gentlemanly player in the league. When Lord and Lady Byng moved back to England, Uncle Barney moved to Montreal where he set up Forum Florists in the Forum, the hockey arena used by the Montreal Canadiens.

Uncle Barney was the only florist in a National Hockey League arena in North America. I wondered whether Lady Byng had a hand in that. My father helped him out there too, and when my dad, now living in Toronto, looked for a business of his own, he understood the flower business and set up Flowerdale Florists.

It wasn't a thriving business. Only two other people worked in my father's flower store in Toronto. Carl was the delivery man and Mrs Henson did some flower arranging but mostly sold flowers and plants to customers. I knew Mr and Mrs Henson had a daughter my age but I never met her until, one Saturday morning, Dad arrived with her. Anna was neat, with long thick blonde hair the colour of peaches and cream. She kept it all in a ponytail, with a white ribbon tied over an elastic hair band and she wore two white barrettes to keep stragglers from getting in her way. I thought her eyes were the colour of a fresh summer sky and that she looked quite fetching.

Mum had explained to us before Anna arrived that her parents were having a holiday and Dad had told Mrs Henson that Anna could stay with us for the week. Mum told Rob and me that Anna had never been to a cottage before. Although she brought a bathing suit and bathing cap with her, she arrived with lots of dresses and not much else. Her brown leather shoes had laces. She didn't have moccasins. This was the first time in her life, she told me, she had been out of Toronto.

It was the middle of summer. The weather was coming from the southwest and I knew it would be hot, hazy and humid, day after day, that one day would just follow the next with no change, even at night. I knew it was good to be out of the city when that happened.

After Anna met the rest of the family, Mum asked me to show her around the cottage. I took her to the dock, the boathouse, the tree house and the bunkhouse where guests usually slept, but because she was so young Mum had decided she'd sleep in the spare room in the cottage and Uncle would move to the bunkhouse.

By the time the tour was over it was time for lunch. Anna asked where she could wash her hands and when she returned she asked my mother what we were having. She was told peanut butter and jam sandwiches and she asked what type of peanut butter. 'Crunchy, dear,' was the answer.

'What type of jam?' she asked.

'Grape jam,' Mum answered.

'What am I drinking?' Anna asked and she was told that as a treat everyone was having fresh-squeezed orange juice.

I was surprised at all these questions. Rob and I ate what we were given. We knew not to ask.

Anna enjoyed her lunch and finished it all.

'I want more orange juice,' she said, lifting her glass from the table in the direction of my mother.

'I want never gets.' That's what my mother always told us when we forgot to say 'Please', but without much ado she refilled Anna's glass although I saw her catch my uncle's eye and her eyebrow rise a little.

After lunch I took Anna to meet Grace. On hot days like that there are always deerflies and horseflies buzzing around, especially if you were swimming in the lake. You just get used to them but Anna screamed and screamed when a horsefly dived around her hair and I had to swipe at it for what seemed an eternity before it left and Anna calmed down.

Grace was lying on her bed in her bunkhouse reading a Nancy Drew book when we arrived. I introduced them and while Anna was looking around the bunkhouse I whispered to Grace, 'I think she's pretty.'

'She isn't,' Grace replied, then she said she had to do something or other for her mother, left the bunkhouse and went into her cottage.

My visitor and I were already partway down the point so I suggested that we walk up to the county road and across it to where the wildflowers were at their most luxurious. Walking up the widened track, I asked Anna, 'Do you believe in God?' and she said, 'Yes, he's everywhere in everyone and everything.'

'My mum says that God can't be everywhere so he made mothers,' I replied.

'He couldn't have made my mother. She hurts me,' Anna said.

When we reached the road I saw something down towards the Nichols' farmhouse and we walked over to investigate. It was a just-run-over garter snake with the last of her young crawling out of her crushed body, slithering towards both sides of the road. Anna held her head with both hands, jumped up and down and screamed.

'Shush!' I told her angrily. I was upset to see the dead mother snake and irritated at Anna for being so uncaring, for showing no respect for the dead mother. I picked up the baby snakes, sometimes two or three at a time, and placed all of them together in the roadside ditch, where the weeds were lush and the ground cooler.

'We'll go back to the cottage now,' I said firmly, after I finished, and walked there so fast Anna had to break into a run now and then to keep up with me.

I hoped that Robert would be at the cottage when we got back but he had gone off to Steve's. Anna said she wanted to unpack and I was relieved to get rid of her. I went to find Uncle Reub who was in the bunkhouse.

'She's come here to bother me. She's very childish,' I said and sat on the end of my uncle's bed.

'She's very demanding,' I continued. 'Her mother hurts her. She's very pretty.'

Uncle looked at me.

'Did she tell you her mother hurts her?' Uncle asked.

'Yes,' I replied.

'Do you want to be her friend? She'd like that,' he said and I shrugged my shoulders.

'She's only here until next weekend. If you want to be a good friend let her say what's on her mind. And if you think she's pretty let her hear you say that about her to others.'

Over the following days, I decided to be good to Anna although I hated her prissiness and her lack of manners with my parents and my uncle. My mother was always saying, 'Examine the contents, not the bottle.' I thought hard about that. Anna was the bottle and the bottle was attractive. The more I looked at Anna the more beautiful I thought she was but the more I examined what was in the bottle the less I liked her. I introduced her to the lake but she hated it. 'The bottom feels icky,' she said.

I showed her crayfish and she said they looked like they were from a horror movie. I showed her how to put a worm on a hook and she screamed and said she would faint if I ever did that again. She was afraid of fish, afraid of frogs, even afraid of ants. I found her increasingly annoying.

Uncle Reub spent as much time that week with Anna as I did. They went for walks together. Uncle Reub never asked my mother to join us when he walked or talked with me, but when he was with Anna he asked Mum to join them and she did. Mum smiled a lot when they talked. She always absently touched people and when she talked with Anna she held her hand or stroked her cheek. Sometimes she had her serious face on and I knew something was troubling her. I asked my uncle what they talked about and he told me they were just letting Anna say what was on her mind.

Before Anna arrived I had thought that each day was new and different but with Anna there I began to think they weren't. I had set routines, checking the shoreline before breakfast, going to frog bog with Perry, rowing with Grace, fighting with Rob, the fathers arriving on weekends. With Anna there that rhythm had changed.

I tried to stick to my routines and was happy that for the rest of the week my uncle spent considerable time with Anna. He told her some of his favourite short stories and also some of his long stories, the ones that meandered every which way but were still fun to listen to.

Grace seemed to keep an eye on Anna. Wherever Anna went, Grace was sure to find her, just to be there. When I took Anna to the abandoned barn, Grace followed. After I gave Anna a helping hand climbing into the hayloft and we sat there talking about nothing much, Grace sat down beside me and held my hand in hers.

On the day before Anna was due to return to the city I decided to row her out to the new diving raft and Grace accompanied us. It was another hot day and for some reason or other the mallard ducks were squawking like nobody's business. My father had bought sections of the old floating bridge and he'd had some of the twelve-inch squared timbers towed by one of the Blewetts' logging boats back to the cottage. He used some bridge timbers to build the foundation for a new dock, and clad it in the smoothest finished pine so we wouldn't get slivers in our feet. In fact almost all the cottagers on the point bought sections of the floating bridge and built new docks from it, solid docks that would withstand the ravages of winter ice and spring storms for decades.

My father bought extra bridge timbers and built a diving raft for all the children on the point to use and clad that too in the finest finished pine. We arrived at the raft and Grace and I went for a swim with our life vests on. We weren't allowed to swim at the raft without them on, unless Rob or Steve or one of the other older children accompanied us. Grace and I played in the water as we always did, splashing each other, grabbing each other around the waist. When we did that we could feel each other's warmth through the cool lake water. But then Anna said she wanted to go back. It was her last full day so I stopped playing and got out of the water and Grace followed.

I stood up to untie the rowboat from the raft, with Grace standing beside me. Anna stood up to get in the rowboat but as she did so Grace said, 'Whoops!' and bumped into me, and I knocked against Anna, who fell in the lake.

'My hair!' was the first thing Anna screamed.

I felt upset, and amused. I didn't like seeing her cry but enjoyed seeing her in the lake, and with her face and hair wet I thought she looked even prettier. I pulled her back onto the raft, wrapped her in my towel and we rowed back to the dock. This time I didn't let Grace row. I rowed.

Uncle was sitting in his lawn chair listening to the radio on a long extension cord from inside the cottage and when he saw how upset Anna was he got up and walked into the cottage with her. Later they both went back outside, to the vegetable patch where they picked and ate every single ripe raspberry. I saw my uncle smiling and Anna laughing.

That evening I lay in bed and before I fell asleep I decided I'd be extra nice to Grace for the rest of the summer.

*

Dad took Anna back with him the next day and during the following week the Provincial Police car from Bridgenorth arrived at the cottage.

'Hello, Mrs Fogle,' the policeman announced as he got out of his car. 'Mrs Nichols' phone isn't working so Mr Fogle phoned me to let you know he won't be here until Saturday evening this week.'

'Did he say why?' my mother asked.

'He's short staffed,' the policeman replied.

'Thank you for letting me know,' Mum replied, and the policeman doffed his cap, returned to his car and backed down the point far faster than I thought he should have.

We had corn on the cob for dinner that evening, the first of the season, but both Mum and Uncle Reub were silent until my uncle said, 'Kid, I think you should explain what's happening.'

My mother told us that Mrs Henson was no longer working at the flower store so Dad had to work that Saturday.

'Aileen, I'm sure Robert and Bruce would like to know why Mrs Henson isn't employed any longer.'

'Children,' my mother began, 'in our family we might get angry and we sometimes say foolish things but we never hit each other. Ever. Especially children. I'm afraid that in other families adults sometimes hit their children and Anna lives in one of those families.'

'How do you know?' Rob asked and our mother explained to us that Anna had talked to her and Uncle Reub about how her parents treated her. Now I knew what Anna meant when she said her mother hurts her.

'We told your father and he's fired Mrs Henson so he has to work this Saturday.'

'Is Dad going to teach her parents a lesson?' Rob asked, and for the first time since the policeman arrived Mum's face softened into a radiant smile.

'Your uncle and I had to physically restrain him.'

'Boys, your father might not say much,' Uncle added, 'but he knows right from wrong. Woe betide anyone who raises a hand to a child.'

Rob washed and I dried the dishes after supper. We didn't often talk with each other when we tidied up but that evening we played 'What if'.

'What if Mr Collis hit you?' Rob asked me.

'Dad would punch him so hard he'd end up on Mr Yudin's front lawn.'

'What if Mr Yudin hits Mum?' I countered.

'He'd have such a sore kisser he'd end up on the other side of the lake.'

'What if Mr Everett comes into the cottage?'

'We'd all punch him so hard he'd end up on the moon.'

THE MONOPOLY GAME

Some summer days were perfectly still on Long Point but more often the wind gently whispered. Even when it spoke softly, the sensitive poplars that lined the gravel road tenderly rustled and I felt good inside when I heard the trees talk that way. But now it was August and sometimes the wind suddenly woke up and then the cedars along the lake crackled and the poplars bellowed and roared.

Rob and Steve were building a raft, while Perry and I were in the shallows skipping stones, when the clouds got angry, then full of wrath. Colour drained from the sky and the summer day quickly turned into shades of grey. Seagulls floated in the air; in the increasing wind they had no need to use energy to keep aloft. Then, in no more than seconds, the horizon across the lake went black.

'Get out of the water NOW!' Mum screamed at us and we did. I listened to the rumbling thunder across the lake and wondered whether bits of the world were breaking off.

Curtains of rain raced across the lake towards the cottage then blasts of powerful wind hit the shoreline, blowing the lawn chairs over and I thought that God was playing his whole orchestra: the whistling wind, the churning waves, the bawling leaves.

Inside the cottage, even with the windows tightly closed, the curtains swelled then fell as if each one was breathing in the storm's energy. We gathered around the dining room table. We got out the Monopoly board but then the lights flickered and went out. That always happened with electrical storms. Outside it was as dark as dusk. Thunder cracks and lightning strikes surrounded the cottage. When storms like this suddenly arrived the whole world got as heavy as lead. Solid rain slid down the front windows. The windows looked like waterfalls. I stared through the picture window but I couldn't see a thing. It was as if the whole world had capsized.

Mum got a flashlight and checked the fuse box but she knew it was a typical power failure. It could be minutes or it could be hours before power was restored. She lit the oil lamps on the dining room table, on top of the piano and on the table in front of the big picture window overlooking the lake, then she sat down in one of the rockers and got out a paperback to read. Her brother sat in the other rocker, looking out the window, although there was nothing much to see what with the driving rain.

'I'm banker,' Rob declared. He always did. He sorted the Monopoly money and property cards into neat piles beside him and the game began. Pretty soon all of us except Steve had acquired property to build houses and hotels on and in no time at all an hour had passed. There was still no power. Mum lit a Coleman stove to boil water for tea for herself and for her brother, and as she did Steve landed on 'Jail' and had neither property to sell nor enough money to get out of jail. He didn't even have a 'get out of jail free' card.

'The bank decides to lend Steven five hundred dollars at no interest,' Robert said and I exploded in fury, 'You're cheating! You always cheat. You never help me. He's got no money so he stays in jail!'

'I'm the banker – Iris – and I can lend money to whoever I want,' Rob replied.

One day that spring, as our father was driving us to school I'd told him that I thought the blue irises in our back garden were pretty. From that day on, Rob called me Iris, never Bruce, until a few days before going to the cottage for the summer, when Dad said to Robert, 'Enough of that now.'

Rob knew exactly how I would respond when he called me Iris and he was already ducking when I threw his Monopoly hotels and houses at him and stomped off, hiding my tears.

'That's it,' Mum said. 'Game over until you're civil with each other.'

Perry went into the kitchen, put corn kernels into the screened popper and started making popcorn on the Coleman. I was in my bedroom when my uncle came in.

'I've got a story. Why not come and listen? You don't have to sit near Robert.'

Perry came back with hot popcorn and a bag of pretzels, and while the three other boys sat around the dining room with Uncle Reub, I came out of my bedroom and sat on the nearby sofa.

'Uncle, is this one of your North Dakota stories?' Steve asked.

'Yes it is,' Uncle replied and he sat down with us and started his story.

'Beyond the trees in the land of the ghosts,' he began, but before he got further Robert said, 'Uncle Reub, can you make the story short instead of long?'

'Fine,' he replied. 'Would you like to hear about the turtle who, like a wise woman, hears many things but says nothing?'

Rob and Steve groaned.

'How about how the Mighty Spirit painted spots on the fawn to protect it while it was young?'

'Tell us a story about Indians,' Perry said.

'All right,' Uncle replied and looking at me he said, 'This is a story about how you might think you're not strong but in fact you really are,' and he began.

'One warm summer a beautiful Indian woman was pregnant and about to give birth. She lived in an exquisite tepee where she kept everything in immaculate order but her husband was seldom there. He was a young chief and had better things to do than spend time with his pregnant wife.'

'I thought chiefs are always old,' Robert interrupted.

'Yes, there are paramount chiefs who are old but there are also young chiefs who lead the hunts and war parties. The beautiful woman's chief was a young chief and he had many things to do – cut trees to make poles for the tepee, rebuild the canoe, fish for food, protect his family.

'The beautiful Indian woman was proud to be married to such an eminent man. He was certainly the strongest and the handsomest of all the men in the village but even so she was unhappy and fretted. When she talked with the other wives in the village they all seemed happy with their husbands, even if they weren't as powerful or as handsome as her husband was.

'That's not to say that she didn't know her husband cared for her. He had just finished painting bear paws on the skins of their tepee to stop the arrows of renegade Indians and right now he was down by the lake lashing flint heads to shafts of wood to turn into arrows to shoot deer for dinner. So she consulted the tribe's medicine man whose name was More Clever Than He Thinks.

'If the medicine man had been younger,' Uncle explained to us boys, 'she would have called him More Clever or just More but keeping to formality she asked, "More Clever Than He Thinks, my husband is always busy making things for the tribe, hunting for the tribe, protecting the tribe but soon I will produce a child for him. What can I do to ensure he spends time with his child and with me?"

'The medicine man looked at this fine-looking woman and was reminded that he too had once been married to a gorgeous raven-haired brunette.

'"The land is the mother of all people," he told her, "but you will be the mother of his own son. Name him well, and as he grows ensure his name speaks to his father."

'Boys,' Uncle said, 'Indians can have many names, play names, formal names that are given to them, formal names they give themselves once they're grown up and have taken part in hunts or war parties. That's what the medicine man meant when he told the pregnant woman to ensure her child's name speaks to the father.

'Soon after, the beautiful woman gave birth to a healthy baby boy and gave him the name Best By Far. She fed him well, sewed handsome clothes for him, taught him how to swim and spear fish and recognise the sounds of the woods. Her husband continued to do all the things chiefs need to do, hunt, fish, trap, but she could see, even if he didn't spend his time with her, he was proud of how she was raising his son. As the boy grew she gave him a more formal name, Like Father Like Son. The other boys in the village made fun of these names and called him Minnow because he was small but he knew he had his parents' love.

'One day the boy and his father were standing in the lake looking for fish to spear when a massive muskie – as big as an alligator – crept up behind his father. As its sharp-toothed jaws opened and it was about to eat his father, the boy threw his spear into the muskie's mouth. That spear prevented the giant muskellunge from shutting its mouth and it swam off never again to eat another Indian.

'The handsome father turned to his son and said, "Now you are a man. It is time for you to choose your own name. What will it be?"

'The boy thought for a while and said, "It will be Minnow."

'"But you can give yourself a powerful name," his father replied. "You can be Son Who Saved Father or Muskie Slayer. Why call yourself Minnow?"

'And the boy replied, "Because you taught me to hunt quietly and that surprise is best."'

Like most summer storms, the one that day passed in a shorter time than it would have taken to play a complete Monopoly game. Nature's orchestra went silent. I walked outside by myself, where everything somehow seemed more vivid, more pure. The cottage sparkled and glowed in the sunless ozone. I knew my uncle had been speaking to me.

THE SHOT DOG

I t was Saturday and I had been up for a sunrise more fiery
red than Mr Fitzpatrick's Cadillac. 'Red sky in the morning,
sailor's warning,' Mum had said to no one in particular then,
'I hope we don't have another lightning storm later today. I
phoned Camp Cleveland from Mrs Nichols'. It's pickerel
tonight. We're taking Steven and Perry.'

'I'm going to Beaver Lumber,' my father replied.

'You'll take Bruce with you,' she said and I felt excited. I
knew Dad would be visiting more than the lumberyard.

In the middle of summer there were always tent caterpillars in
the trees along the county road, but that summer there was a
plague of them. I had once asked Uncle Reub why there were so
many apple and crab apple trees along the concession roads but
not in the woods and he said, 'You might hear that Johnny
Appleseed travelled along all the concession roads in Ontario,

spreading apple and crab apple seeds that he'd brought from England, but that's not true. The true answer is more wonderful than that. Birds planted all those trees. They love the sugar in fruit and carry fruit seeds wherever they fly. If you give them a line to settle on, a hydro line, a telephone wire, a wire fence, a cedar fence, that's where they poop most of those seeds. That's why there are so many raspberry stalks along the fences. And that's why the apple trees are on the concession roads.'

Each summer some of the trees that grew from those seeds had caterpillar tents on them, silky caterpillar homes built where tree branches forked, but this year there were so many pests the apple and crab apple trees had already lost almost all of their leaves to the voracious foragers. Wild cherry, ash, birch, willow, witch hazel, poplar, maple, even oak trees were smothered in tents. Worst of all, the new peach, plum and Northern Spy apple trees Dad had planted behind the cottage were infested. At night the caterpillars crawled out of their tents and ate the leaves. My father was going to kill those caterpillars that weekend. He planned to blowtorch their tents to death.

Our first stop was Beaver Lumber where we loaded the station wagon with eight sheets of four-by-eight-foot knotty pine plywood to finish the interior walls of the bunkhouse with. By the time we got to Canadian Tire, to buy a new propane cylinder for the blowtorch, grey clouds, the colour of old nickels, filled the sky. Dad walked up and down all the hardware aisles at the store. I spent my time looking at fishing tackle.

On our way back we stopped at the ice house in Bridgenorth. That was my favourite place in the village. The wooden front was level with the ground but the back of the ice house was built partly into the side of the hill and that's where the ice was stacked, covered in wet sawdust. On other buildings, pinewood siding weathered to an ethereal silver. The ice house's wooden walls were black as ink. Inside was always moist and cool with the same sweet syrupy smell I loved so much at the lumberyard.

Using his ice tongs the iceman lifted a block of Lake Chemong ice from the sawdust it was buried in and carried it to the car where it only just fit on top of the plywood.

'Did he cut the ice last winter himself?' I asked my father.

'Himself. Probably last February,' was the answer. 'He's a strong man. There's his ice-cutting saw and picks,' Dad said, pointing to a band saw with serrated teeth as big as a shark's. 'He used those ice picks to pull the blocks out of the lake. Then he put them on a flat freight sleigh and borrowed the Blewetts' tractor to get it here.'

It was drizzling by the time we left the ice house, but it was muggy so we left the car windows partly open. There was just one more stop, at Mr Everett's farm to buy more corn. I heard that like other farmers in that part of the country, Clarence Everett tried everything to make his land productive, egg layers, swine, dairy and beef cattle, silage corn, barley, rye, red Fife wheat, Christmas trees, pumpkins, linseed, now sunflowers. Farmers like Clarence Everett grew barley, wheat and rye for milling but as often as not all they got for their hard labour was animal feed. Now he was trying corn on the cob, to sell to local grocery stores and direct to the summer people.

As we drove up the tree-lined drive from the county road and slowed as we approached the farmhouse I heard a noise, *ka-pow*, then a yelp that cut into my heart, then again *ka-pow, ka-pow*.

Dad gunned the car's engine and shot past the farmhouse, skidding to a stop in front of the barn, where he threw open his door and, standing as straight as a hydro pole and as big as a grizzly bear, he shouted, 'Stop that!'

I stayed in the car. I wanted to see what was happening but was frightened by my father's sudden anger, a rage I'd never seen before. I watched through the front window as Dad marched over to Clarence Everett. I heard shouting but I couldn't make out what they were barking at each other. I worried because even though Dad was bigger than the farmer, Mr Everett was holding a rifle. The men waved their arms and bellowed for what seemed forever, then Dad stopped shouting and gesticulating, got down on one knee, picked up a big, limp brown dog and carried it back to the car. I knew that dog and called him Brownie, although I never knew his real name. He accompanied the farmer's cattle when they ambled along the highway and sometimes came to our cottage to see what Angus was up to.

'Bruce, open the tailgate,' my father demanded, which I did, and Dad pushed the block of ice forward, laid the dog's lifeless body on the plywood, slammed the tailgate shut and we both got back in the station wagon.

My father started the engine then sat with both hands on the steering wheel, going nowhere, saying nothing. I felt all mixed up inside and didn't know what to say. I worried that Mr Everett had a rifle and might kill us too, but then Dad suddenly threw the car into reverse, spun it around and sped back to the county road so fast he almost landed the car in the ditch when he finally braked. Again, he sat with his hands on the steering wheel, going nowhere, saying nothing and then, loud and crisp he said, 'The bastard!'

He didn't look at me. He didn't look at the dead dog in the back of the car, he just sat there then said, 'Bastard!' again.

I was more shocked than when I heard Grace swear. My

father hated swearing, more than almost anything, and now he was doing what he told his children we must never do. All of a sudden he turned the car onto the asphalted road, so fast that even in the wet the car's tyres squealed for an eternity, and he raced back to the cottage.

It was raining harder when we got home. Dad and I, still saying nothing to each other, got out of the car and walked into the cottage.

'Everett just killed his dog,' Dad said to Mum.

When he heard that, Uncle Reub got up from his rocking chair and walked over. Robert, Steven and Perry stopped playing triple solitaire, looked at the adults and said nothing.

'I'm burying him in the field,' Dad said.

Of course, when my father felt something needed to get done it got done there and then, so he went to the tool house for his rain poncho and a spade, and us four boys silently and excitedly followed him. We too got out our waterproofs and slipped them over our heads. By the time we returned to the car, Uncle Reub was there, sheltering under the black umbrella.

Dad opened the tailgate, stared at the dog for only seconds then lifted it from the car.

'Morris, before you bury him, may I show the boys something?' Uncle asked, and seeing acceptance in his brother-in-law's eyes, asked him to carry the body to the front of the cottage and place it under the tree house where we would all be protected from the rain.

'I'll bring it back once we're finished,' he said, and my father busied himself removing his purchases from the car.

'Boys, let's have a look,' Uncle Reub said, and we gathered under the tree house around the brown dog's flaccid body. He lifted the dog's head and it hung like a wilted flower. To us it looked as if the dog was only sleeping, but for the blood seeping from its nostrils and mouth. Whenever I accidentally cut myself I thought my blood was beautiful, but this blood dripping from the dog's nose wasn't. When Rob saw that blood he turned away.

Uncle Reub ran his small firm hands deftly back and forth over the dog's rib cage then its belly then back to the ribs. When he finished both hands were blood stained.

'It's been shot with a high-velocity rifle,' he said. 'See this? There's almost nothing to see here, just a little hair pulled into these three small holes. That's where the bullets entered his chest. See here? On the other side? That large hole is where all the bullets left the body. This dog was shot up close through the heart by a good marksman.'

We were riveted. We squatted in a semicircle around the dog, bending over it as Uncle Reub rolled the floppy body on its back so that the dog's limbs hung limply away, then from his back pocket he took a leather case, unzipped it and withdrew a scalpel and a pair of scissors.

'The rain has helped. It will be easier to do a proper post-mortem if hair doesn't get in the way,' and saying nothing more he made a single long incision through the dog's skin from its chest to its hips.

'I'm going to puke,' Rob said and he meant it. He never even gutted fish he caught, he left that for me to do and, now, to see an animal so much like his own dog being cut open was too much, and he ran into the cottage.

'I'll leave the chest closed,' Uncle continued. 'It's filled with blood and the heart has been turned to pulp by the bullets. What's fascinating, boys, is that the lungs will be good, just tracks where the bullets went through them. High-velocity bullets turn organs like liver or spleen or heart into hamburger.'

'What's different about the lungs?' I asked, and my uncle explained that because they were so elastic they stretched then snapped back to normal when pierced by bullets. 'Like spider's web, bullets just pass through it. Other tissue doesn't behave like that.'

I peered closer.

Uncle Reub made another swift incision with his scalpel blade along the dog's belly, this time through the muscle wall, and intestines ballooned out over its hair.

'I'm going to see how Rob is,' Steve said, as the intestines settled in coils over the side of the dog, and he left the shelter under the tree house and returned to the cottage.

'What's that red thing?' Perry asked. Uncle explained it was the dog's spleen. He pulled more intestines out until they all lay on the dog's fur then he spread open the now emptied cavity and asked Perry and me to look in.

'Are you looking for its soul?' I asked.

'Good question. Some people think only humans have souls,' he answered. 'Personally, I think if we have them so do dogs, but it isn't part of the anatomy so, boys, I can't show it to you.'

'There's a kidney,' he said. 'It makes urine that travels down that tube there to the bladder, where it's stored until the dog needs to pee.' He showed us the dog's bladder.

'Here's the stomach and if you look up there under the ribs that's the liver. It cleans the blood and filters out anything unpleasant the dog has eaten. Food goes into the intestines here,' and he showed us where the intestines began. 'There's a muscle that holds food in the stomach until it's ready to go into the intestines.'

'May I feel it?' I asked, and both Perry and I ran our fingers over the still-warm stomach and intestines.

'Run the intestines through your fingers and you'll see how long they are.'

We did, four hands inspecting it inch by inch.

'Food is digested in the small intestine and once it gets past that thing,' he pointed to the appendix, 'it enters the large intestine where moisture is removed and all that's left is faeces.'

He paused and looked at us. We couldn't take our eyes off the dog's innards.

'Boys, we are no different inside to this dog. If you become doctors this is your meat and potatoes. Now, let's tidy up for your father,' and he asked me to get my mother's sewing box from the cottage, which I did. With a doubled strand of black cotton and a long straight needle, and asking us to squeeze the intestines back into the belly as he worked, he sewed up his incision with such deftness that when he finished it looked as if nothing had ever been done to that dog.

'Tell your father we can bury him now,' and to our surprise Uncle Reub picked up the dog's body himself and, mindless that it was soiling the white shirt he was wearing and oblivious to the rain, he carried the body around to the back of the cottage and beyond to the field where Dad had already dug a grave. Bending down he got on one knee, then the next, and gently lowered the brown dog into the black earth.

Dad had already started to shovel earth into the grave before I thought there should be a ceremony.

'Shouldn't we say a prayer?' I asked. My father looked at his brother-in-law and knew he should stop.

When Grace and I found the dead heron and I'd made a cross for its grave, Grace had asked me how I knew it was Christian. I had thought that was a dumb question. 'Everything's Christian,' I'd told her, and I said a Christian prayer for it. But now I was thinking maybe some things aren't Christian. Maybe some things are Indian.

I moved to the edge of the grave, looked down at what I thought was, even in death, an elegant and beautiful animal and said, 'Grandmother earth, we return this dog to you. The sun gave this dog its life. The sun will enter the earth and keep it warm for this dog,' and I stepped back and let my dad continue shovelling back the earth he had dug.

Perry asked me where I heard that prayer and I told him I made it up as I spoke.

'Stop!' I shouted. Another thought had entered my mind and I asked Uncle Reub for his pocket knife, then in the drizzle raced across the narrow field up to the county road, past the brick house to the next field where I cut off a sunflower head and ran back with it. By the time I got there Perry had become bored and gone back in the cottage. I put the sunflower head in the grave, Dad completed filling the hole, and the two grown men and I returned to the cottage.

There was no lightning that day so the drive over the causeway to Pigeon Lake for our pickerel meal at the fishing camp was uneventful and the meal was good. By the time we returned to the cottage the rain had stopped. I took a flashlight, went outside and sat by the shot dog's grave until Mum asked me to come back in for bed. That night, I asked Angus to crawl under the covers with me and he stayed, sleeping by my calf, all night.

At dawn the next day, I returned to the grave. Dad was already at work blowtorching the caterpillar tents in the peach tree.

I knew a sunflower couldn't grow overnight but deep in my heart I had hoped that this time there would be magic. I sat by the grave for a few minutes then returned to the cottage. Each day for the next three weeks I went to the dog's grave each morning before breakfast and said a special prayer for it. By the end of the summer, sweet peas that had seeded themselves nearby covered the dog's grave.

SMOKED SALMON

One August weekend Grace's father took his family to Algonquin Park for a five-day canoe trip and I felt miserable. Grace had not come over to say goodbye to me.

Grace had told me how exciting it was that they were going camping and the afternoon before, while Grace and I were swimming together by her dock, I had seen her father lift their canoe from the lake and carry it over his shoulders up to his Oldsmobile. Grace said they might not go. Her mother wasn't feeling well.

Now they had gone and, even though there were lots of cars behind the other cottages and it was another blue summer day, I felt empty, the way I felt when they left the cottage for the last time at the end of summer.

Rob told me he was going up to Cedar Bay then they were all going to the fort but I didn't join my brother. I loved the fort but hated what the other boys did there. Last time, Steve siphoned gas from his boat's gas tank and put some in an oil can he had removed the top from. At the fort they tossed a match in the can, then frogs, and bet which frog made the most jumps before it burned to death. I told Grace about what the boys did at the fort and that made me feel better, just talking to her about it. In fact I felt better spending my days with her than with my brother or the other boys. It was sunny every day, even when it rained, when I was with her.

I spent the morning on my bed doing nothing much – staring at the ceiling – then just before lunch I decided I'd collect some clay. I walked outside and the sandpipers bobbing their tails up and down on the shore flew away when the screen door slammed behind me. A seagull I called Popeye watched me from the dock. From the start of summer I left sandwich crusts on the dock and this gull had become so relaxed, now it walked right up to me begging for food. Uncle Reub was in his lawn chair and had been watching the sandpipers.

Over the summer I had gradually come to realise that my uncle was somehow different to the other grown-ups. When any of us children talked to him he really listened. He was different that way. But there was also something missing, something empty about him. I looked at my uncle, sitting alone, his brown eyes reflecting the summer glow off the lake, and it seemed that his face had been washed of all expression. That wasn't how he had always been. Two years before, when he returned from the United States to Toronto in a canary-yellow convertible, and was married to Samantha who was half a foot taller than him and so pretty she looked like a movie star, his eyes twinkled, the way they still did when he told us stories.

'It's funny,' I said. 'The more you like someone the less they like you back.'

'That's very profound, Bruce,' my uncle replied. 'So what do you do?'

'I guess you just keep on liking them. You can't help it,' I said.

My uncle sighed, looked out at the lake then looked me in the eyes.

'That's very true,' he said ever so slowly and I knew his thoughts were racing from here to there and back here again, like whirlwinds dancing on the lake.

We didn't say any more but from that moment I felt closer to my uncle than anyone else, that with him I could say what I really felt.

Using a trowel I started digging a wide hole in the sun-dried, ochre-coloured sand. The warm sand was muddy brown and digging deeper the excavation soon started to fill with water, but it wasn't warm lake water, it was as cold as ice. A natural spring, only feet below the surface of the beach, fed into the lake right in front of the cottage. I dug further, through the cold water until my trowel reached clay, sticky, freezing cold clay, so thick it was almost impossible to dig up. Now I had to use all my strength, to push the trowel as deep as possible into the clay then lift it up through the cold muddy pool. I collected five trowels full of clay, washing the sand off each load by swishing it in the lake and stroking my hand all over it until it felt as soft and smooth as Grace's arm. I collected the clay in a tin bucket, covered it with a wet cloth and put it in the shade of one of the cedar trees.

At lunchtime, Mum brought our lunch outside and we ate at the garden table. Dad had brought a whole side of smoked salmon from the city.

'Kid, you make the best smoked salmon sandwiches on the whole lake,' my uncle told his sister, then he turned to me.

'Do you know that smoked salmon played an important role in Canada's history?'

I had food in my mouth so I raised my eyebrows instead of answering.

'The Americans think that Lewis and Clark were the first white men to cross the continent but it was a Canadian from Montreal, Alexander Mackenzie, who did, ten years before the Americans.'

'Why do the Americans think they were first?' I asked.

'Because Alexander Mackenzie used Indians to help him. He left Montreal and travelled through one tribe's land after another, hiring guides who spoke the language of the next tribe. He passed north of here and might have employed one of Mr Muskratt's ancestors to guide him.'

'What's smoked salmon got to do with it?' I asked.

'Well, Brucie, the first time he tried to cross the continent he hired one guide who was all talk but not much knowledge who took him the wrong way, but it turned out OK because Mackenzie discovered the Arctic Ocean. He had to spend the winter somewhere near Great Slave Lake. Next summer he hired better guides and kept on walking and canoeing. He was just about to give up when he met a tribe that offered him smoked salmon like this so he knew he was near the Pacific and kept going.'

As lunch finished Uncle said, 'Let's walk off lunch and I'll tell you a story.' We walked up to the road behind the cottages, past Grace's cottage that looked unhappy and forlorn, at least that's what I thought.

'Brucie, while I was having lunch I was thinking that that salmon and I are similar. You know how your mother says, "Distant fields always look greener," that's what we both thought, the salmon and me. That salmon – it came from the

Atlantic Ocean, not the Pacific – that salmon, while it was alive, its life was like mine. It was a restless fish. It didn't realise how good a life it had and that's how it ended up on our plates instead of swimming free in the Atlantic.'

We reached the end of Long Point where my uncle and I sat down on a pile of granite boulders that had been cleared a hundred years before from the adjacent field. I picked some toadflax to play with, squeezing the snapdragon-like flowers to open them, counting the ants walking around inside.

'Isn't that interesting,' my uncle said, 'in North Dakota, Scandinavian farmers boil toadflax and put the liquid in glass bottles for attracting and poisoning flies.' Then he continued.

'On the farm where I grew up near Whitby, our family had everything, milk from the cows, eggs from the chickens. Cabbage. Pickles. That salmon also grew up in the most wonderful place in the world, on the Restigouche River in New Brunswick, but one day, after he had become an adult, he had an urge to leave so he did. He set out for a bigger world, a better world and he thrived in his new world. I did too. He grew into a powerful silver salmon. After I graduated in medicine I went to the United States. Do you know I have a commendation signed by President Roosevelt?'

I shook my head 'no', but said nothing. I wanted to hear what happened next.

'Well, that salmon, amongst all the great riches of the sea, with all he would ever need, that restless salmon felt a powerful urge to give all of that up and go back home. So he did. From the vastness of the Atlantic Ocean he found his way back to New Brunswick, back to the Restigouche River. With his powerful body he nobly swam up that river, back to the place of his birth. He almost got there but in sight of where he was born and raised, a fisherman netted and killed him. That fisherman took him the same day to a smokery where he was smoked over logs from sugar maple trees for a few days then he was packed in ice and sent by train to Toronto where your father bought him, then your mother cut him into thin slices and after there's nothing left of him she'll feed his silvery skin to Angus.'

'But what's the same with you?' I asked, and Uncle Reub continued.

'That salmon felt a need to migrate but it didn't help. He was never comfortable wherever he was. So he returned home, hoping he would feel better back there. Bruce, it's good to return to places where you've been happy – or even sad. Even if the people that made it happy or sad are never there again, even if the buildings are gone, it's good to return. In Mandan, I felt like that salmon. My wife wanted to stay but I told her we had to leave. Soon after we returned here she left me for another man.'

I didn't say anything at first. Instead I picked more toadflax but then I asked, 'Is that why you always look sad?' and my uncle quietly replied, 'Yes it is.'

'Is that why you're here instead of at your own home?' I asked.

'Yes it is.'

My questions continued, 'Is that why my mother takes care of you?'

My uncle replied, 'You know I'm twenty years older than your mother, old enough to be her father but yes, she mothers me,' and then he said, 'Do you miss Grace?'

I answered, 'Yes I do.'

We both sat with our backs hunched to the sun and said no more for a while, until my uncle said, 'When you're an adult, Bruce, and you think back to your summers here, all you'll remember are the good things. I promise you that. You'll forget how sad you feel today.'

I didn't say anything. All I did was pull spikes of plantain out of the soil at my feet, gathering the stalks in one hand until my uncle asked, 'Do you know that women smile a lot more at people like the milkman and bread man than men do?' and that made me grin.

We walked back to the cottage. I spent the afternoon making clay perch. Uncle Reub asked my father to drive him into Bridgenorth for a shave and a haircut. Of course my dad did. He always did anything anyone asked. While in town my uncle visited the General Store where he bought a coloured shirt for himself and a Lazy Susan for the dining-room table for his sister.

THE BUNKHOUSE

A simple smell brings back sights, sounds, even tastes. I wondered why I was so good at smelling things but I never had the words to describe what I smelled. I couldn't remember exactly what my Grade One schoolteacher looked like. I couldn't remember what her voice sounded like either but when I smelled someone wearing the perfume she wore I was instantly taken back to exactly where I sat in her classroom, who sat next to me, even the sound of chalk on the blackboard. How can a smell, I wondered, trigger such memories?

Our bunkhouse had a lovely smell all of its own. I recognised that it shared part of its smell with the lumberyard but it had its own unique smell, different to the cottage, different from the smell of Grace's bunkhouse.

THE BUNKHOUSE

The bunkhouse was a later addition that Dad built to accommodate weekend guests. It sat, squat and white, at the back of the cottage where us boys once played badminton when the cottage was first built. There was no window to the east to catch the morning sun, only a small one to the south opening onto the new row of poplars, another small one to the west facing the cottage and two to the north overlooking the lawn. They all had screens on them and short cotton curtains inside.

After Anna had returned to the city, I was in my bedroom when I'd overheard my mother and my uncle arguing in the kitchen about something or other. It wasn't that their voices were raised. They just sounded more tense. When I concentrated on what was happening I heard my uncle say, 'Kid, I'm old enough to sleep on my own.' I thought that was funny, that only children would say something like that. 'You should be with people,' I heard my mother reply. Soon after Uncle Reub bought himself his new bright shirt, when my father had finished the interior walls of the bunkhouse with new plywood and put the rag rugs and old Persian carpets back on the floor, and the bunkhouse's old smell returned, my uncle had returned to it and slept there each night for the remainder of the summer.

The day after Grace came back from Algonquin Park was bright and crystal clear but fiercely windy and unseasonably cold. Steven and Perry's mother had driven down from Cedar Bay and taken my mother and uncle over to a friend's cottage for the afternoon. Grace and I tried to escape from the cold wind by going to the woods but it was cold there too and we returned to my bunkhouse where we lay on the big bed and watched a corner of light edge its way along a window sill. Both of us felt good lying on the bed together.

'That chipmunk is so annoying!' Grace said. There was a busy scurrying of feet back and forth over the plywood ceiling above us.

'It's storing seeds for the winter,' I explained.

Grace replied, 'Well, it should do it somewhere else,' and she folded her arms over her chest.

Early in summer I had learned something I thought quite important, and that was that the best way for nature to hide was to take on the colours of its surroundings. Black bass weren't really black. They were as green as lake water on top and the colour of a cloud-filled sky on the bottom. The lake was the same. Sometimes it was a perfect reflection of the sky. On overcast days it looked like hammered pewter. Sometimes I heard a chipmunk's chattering but it always took ages before I could pick it out of its perfect camouflage amongst the trees and shrubs.

I actually liked the sound the chipmunk made, as much as I loved the smell of the bunkhouse. I thought my father liked giving needy animals a home – he was always bringing injured wildlife back to the cottage – and the chipmunk had simply taken up the offer and was doing its housekeeping, just like my mother did. In spring, when I returned to the cottage, even though the chipmunks had hibernated in the wall's insulation over winter, I knew there would be piles of nutshells over an inch thick above the ceiling plywood.

'What was the canoe trip like?' I asked.

'I was bored,' my neighbour answered. 'We camped the first night and that was OK but Mummy felt sick and Daddy knows Mr Kates, so we stayed at his hotel but I wasn't allowed to visit his summer camp.'

'What did you do then?' I enquired with a genuine curiosity, and Grace said she canoed on Little Joe Lake with her sister and fished but not much else.

'I did see a moose,' she continued. 'When we paddled down to the narrows there was a mother moose and her baby standing in the water. She was eating water lilies and her baby was having a drink of milk. That was neat.'

'What did you do?' I asked and Grace told me they just floated in their canoe, watching until they got bored and started paddling again, through the narrows into the next lake.

'I saw a moose up at Mud Lake while you were gone,' I told Grace.

She turned her head and stared straight into my eyes, just inches away, and it took only seconds before I couldn't look at her any longer and turned away.

'I don't believe that,' she said.

My mother was always saying, 'Believe half of what you hear but be wise enough to know which half,' and I wondered how on earth Grace knew I was lying.

Before I could admit I'd lied, Grace said, 'Did you miss me?' and I replied, 'Sort of.'

She moved closer to me until our shoulders touched. Grace didn't need perfume. She had her own sweet smell and I thought it was just perfect. We spent the afternoon lying on the big bed, staring at the ceiling, watching flies walk on it, talking about this and that, until Grace got bored and went home for supper.

THE MALLARD

Each spring the mallards returned to the lake long before the summer people did, sometimes so early the lake was still frozen and the only water to stand in or drink from was melt water in hollows in the fields. The ducks were there in May when my father and I had dug the vegetable patch, squawking and quacking and being all dramatic about who'd mate with who. Their urges were so great some of the males, when they failed to find a female, tried mating with other males. By summer the ducks were more civilised. Sometimes I saw flocks of males hanging out together on the lake. At other times I saw pairs, a fluorescent green-headed male with his rather non-descript speckled brown female, paddling in unison this way or that. More often I saw single females and I knew they had eggs somewhere nearby.

From the day I arrived at the cottage I walked the shoreline. I looked for changes from the previous summer, trees that had fallen or wooden docks that winter ice had torn from the shore and spring storms had impaled into the cedar trees. I looked for treasure – fishing line, life jackets, oars, wooden lures, beautiful driftwood. Right through summer I patrolled the shoreline and in late July I found a new mallard's nest in thick grass and black raspberry canes less than ten feet from the shoreline by the marsh just beyond the new neighbour's never-used boathouse.

The nest wasn't much – a depression in the grass, bits of weeds and rushes, some fluffy belly feathers. When I stared at those downy feathers long enough, they became winter mountains, their soft curves covered in snow.

Each day the number of eggs increased. I couldn't decide whether they looked slightly green because of the lushness of the surrounding grass or really were a dull green. By the time she had finished I thought there were nine eggs. I didn't know because from that time on, whenever I approached she was always nesting on them, never moving, even when I quietly crept near her. She didn't seem to mind my being there and was as tame to my presence as Popeye the seagull was.

One Saturday in early August my father had nothing else to do so he decided to install an old porcelain bathroom sink, complete with running hot and cold water, in the cedar hedge by the lake. By the time I saw what he was doing Dad had dug trenches and laid in rubber pipes.

'What's that for?' I asked and Dad answered, 'To wash your hands after fishing.' I thought that I could do as I'd always done and wash my hands in the lake but I didn't say so.

'I'm going to the ducks,' I said to no one in particular and Uncle Reub, who was sitting on his lawn chair watching his brother-in-law install the sink, asked if he could come along and I was happy he had asked. I was proud of my find and wanted to show the mallard nest to my uncle.

The night had been windy and the shore was a tangle of seaweed and driftwood so we walked along the grassy shoreline rather than through the shallows. We stopped at the patch of black raspberries and ate all the ripe ones we could find. While we were there I found an exquisite feather and handed it to my uncle. It was in perfect condition, shades of grey that abruptly changed to yellow at the tip, as if someone had painted sunshine on it. Uncle stroked the soft feather towards the tip, then ran his fingers back towards the small quill. 'Bruce,' he said, 'I know this sounds mad but a woman is just like this fine-looking feather – it's a cedar waxwing's feather so there's probably a flock of them nearby, here for the berries. They're both beautiful and alluring but they're both unforgiving if you stroke them the wrong way.'

I was more interested in presenting the mallard's nest to my uncle, so I walked over to the nest with my uncle following me but when we arrived it was empty. The mother and her eggs were gone. I was sure a mink had killed and eaten them but when I looked through the bulrushes, into the purple pickerelweed, pond lilies and wapato, there they all were, the mother and her ducklings. The eggs had hatched and she had successfully led them to the safety of the marshy waters.

Uncle Reub and I walked to the edge of the still marsh, its waters protected from southerly winds by a peninsula and from northerly winds by the long dock beside the neighbour's boathouse. Stepping from one granite boulder to another I walked out into the marsh as far as I could. It was hard to count them, I had to start over and over, but finally I counted thirteen ducklings, wet little balls of feathers with brown backs spotted with yellow, and bright yellow faces. Their mother was silent – not a quack from her.

*

Each day for the next three days my uncle and I returned to the marsh and watched the mother and her ducklings dabble. Uncle explained that mallards were mostly vegetarian, that they fed on seeds and berries, wild rice and leaves and bulrushes, but they were also happy to eat tadpoles and fish eggs, worms, insects, even small fish or frogs when they were plentiful. He told me how that mother duck used her bill to filter food from mud at the edges of the marsh.

He corrected me about something that I had got wrong. I thought there were two different types of ducks squawking on the lake but there weren't. It was just that female mallards quacked like farmyard ducks but male mallards made the softer, lower-pitched sound I sometimes heard. Uncle explained that mallard pairs always returned, or at least tried to return, to their previous nesting site. 'Your parents are much like those mallards, Brucie, returning to your cottage each summer. It makes me feel good, seeing this rhythm of life.'

On the fourth day, we didn't go to the marsh because the mother had brought her brood out onto the lake and they were paddling near the shore in front of our cottage.

'Watch Popeye,' Uncle advised me. 'He might like one of those ducklings for breakfast.'

Popeye didn't show the slightest interest but, to be safe, when Popeye was floating in the water or standing on the dock, I always waded out so that I was between Popeye and the ducklings. The ducklings and their mother didn't mind me. On one occasion a brave duckling paddled right over to me and pecked at my bathing suit.

When he was back at the cottage the following weekend, I proudly showed the thirteen ducklings to my dad, and explained that I was in the lake because I was protecting them from being eaten by Popeye, who was standing on the dock. Angus wasn't a problem. He never took any interest in birds, only mammals.

The air was perfectly still and the lake so calm it looked as if I was standing in a giant puddle of mercury. I was intently watching Popeye when suddenly a tidal wave surged towards the ducklings and there was a ferocious splash. When the waves subsided and I counted the brood there were only twelve.

'Goodness gracious,' Dad exclaimed. 'That was a muskie!'

'No,' I shouted. 'That's not fair!'

Uncle got up from his chair and walked to the shore. The mother mallard just kept dabbling and the brood that had fled in all directions reformed and crowded their mother.

My first thought was that it couldn't be a muskie. There weren't any rocky drop-offs or sand bars in front of the cottage. No one ever fished for muskies there. And besides, I'd never seen one anywhere near the cottage in my flying dreams. But then I remembered the weed beds, and the time I was paddling the rowboat when a mouth as big as the Loch Ness monster lunged at the end of the rope trailing in the water behind the boat. It must be the same fish. It had to be. That horrible fish had waited motionless until the duckling got close then it lunged and swallowed the defenceless duckling whole, and alive.

'It's just not fair,' I said once more as I walked, with slumped shoulders from the lake.

'No,' Uncle Reub replied. 'It's not fair but that's the way the world is. The strong devour the weak.'

'I don't mean that,' I replied, for my mind had wandered from the duckling to its mother.

'She did nothing. She didn't care. It's as if nothing happened. If God made mothers because he can't be everywhere then why isn't she at least sad,' and as I talked I dried my legs with a beach towel and sat down on the grass.

Uncle was silent for a moment. 'She might have tears in her heart but she doesn't want to show them. That sometimes happens,' he replied. 'She knows that life – it goes on, for her and for the rest of her brood. Maybe she thinks to herself, "OK, that was sickening but now it's the past. I need to look after the rest of my brood. Myself too." Maybe she thinks the most important thing is to get on with life.'

I thought about that for a moment, then said, 'I'm going over to Grace's.'

THE TENT

The tent was made of oiled canvas and even when the sun was not beating down on it, the air inside was syrupy sweet. It was a small tent, so small you had to crawl on all fours to get in. Grown-ups found that difficult but Uncle didn't. He was already small. Rob and Steve were growing so fast they were now taller than he was. Sometimes Uncle Reub and I would sit in the tent together, one on either side, talking about whatever came into our minds. When Grace joined us she sat beside me.

Dad set up the tent on the front lawn as soon as summer began and it stayed there until he took it down just before we returned to the city at the end of August. At first only the older boys were allowed to sleep overnight under canvas, but by mid-August the parents had relented and when the weather was fair and the night sky sprinkled with sugar they agreed that the younger children could spend the night in it.

At the beginning of summer it had seemed to me that my uncle wanted to separate himself from the world around him. He'd said little – nothing at all to my father – and only talked to my mother when she talked to him. He did little with his days, sitting, reading, sitting with a big book but not reading, although he was funny and interesting and told stories when there were children to talk to. 'Thanks, Kid' was all he'd say when my mother brought him a sandwich at lunchtime or a sweater when the air chilled. When one of the other pretty mothers visited the cottage his face lit up like a rainbow. That's how it looked when he was in the tent. Shiny as an orange.

Now, in August, my uncle seemed more cheerful even when he wasn't in the tent. Now, some mornings he'd sit on his lawn chair and strum his brother-in-law's ukulele, plucking tunes like 'Sweet Georgia Brown' and 'Lover, Come Back to Me'.

One day, while he was playing the ukulele, a terrible thing happened. A ruby-throated hummingbird flew straight into the cottage's big picture window and knocked itself unconscious. I had been watching it, listening to its wings hum as it hovered like a helicopter, taking nectar from the petunias in the blue painted containers in front of the picture window, then it took off and flew straight into the glass.

'Bruce, pick it up gently and take it into the tent,' my uncle told me, and while I did so my uncle fetched honey, water and a glass eye dropper from the cottage. He crawled into the tent and with the dropper he put diluted honey on the bird's long, thin needle-like beak.

'I don't know if this will help but at least we can try,' he said.

I stared intently at the bird, limp in my uncle's hand, and there was no movement.

Eventually my uncle spoke.

'I'm afraid its head injury was too great, Brucie. D-O-A-T, dead on arrival in tent.'

We took the bird from the tent and buried it in the petunia planter where it had just been feeding. This time I felt sad but didn't feel the need for any ceremony and we returned to the sultry warmth of our canvas igloo. Uncle Reub took the ukulele with him.

'Uncle, do you know modern songs?' I asked, and my uncle started to sing.

> *How do I knowwwww*
> *My life is all spent?*
> *My get and go*
> *Has got up and went.*

I lay on my back, looking at the shimmering shadows made by the branches above us. Outside, I could hear the ducks squawking again and carrying on like nobody's business. My uncle had stopped singing but continued strumming chords.

Just as he was saying about the ducks, 'They're singing wedding songs to each other,' Grace crawled in and joined us.

'Your mother knew you were in here,' was all she said and she sat down silent and crossed her arms on her chest.

'Uncle's singing,' I said, but Grace didn't reply.

'Choose a song,' I suggested, but still she didn't talk.

'What's up?' Uncle asked and Grace spat out, 'My mother's decided to have another baby.'

She lay down beside me, pulled her hat over her nose and pretended she was sleeping.

'Isn't that wonderful?' Uncle asked.

'Well, she didn't ask me!' Grace replied. 'She said she'd been praying to God for a baby and now she's pregnant and going to have one.'

'How do you get pregnant?' I asked, and Grace rolled her eyes.

'Hasn't your mother told you?' Grace asked and the truthful answer was that she hadn't.

'I'll talk to your mother later and if she's happy, Brucie, I'll explain everything,' said my uncle.

He turned to Grace and with a very serious look in his eyes he said, 'Grace, she might have a boy. It can be good to have a brother. Do you know you can get pregnant if you swallow a stone?'

'That's stupid. You get pregnant when your husband sleeps near you,' she replied.

'But I know a Sioux Indian woman who fell asleep one evening with a pebble in her mouth and she accidentally swallowed it and got pregnant.'

'Why did she have a pebble in her mouth?' I asked.

'Perhaps she was just hare-brained,' Uncle replied. 'All of us are born childish and some of us remain so. Only that woman knows why she put that pebble in her mouth but nine months later she gave birth to a boy, who she named Stone Boy because his flesh and skin were as hard as granite.'

'Is that why Grace's mother gets sick, because she has a stone in her tummy?' I asked.

'No, dummy. She's sick because she's upset she's upset me,' Grace replied.

'People don't like change,' Uncle Reub said, 'and the woman's two young daughters didn't want another baby in the tepee so she moved far away from her people and raised Stone Boy on her own.

'You see,' Grace said. 'She has a baby and forgets about her family.'

'Grace, the way a story begins is not always the way it ends. Stone is more powerful than anything else on the land but even though he was made of such powerful material his good mother gave her son some special things, a charm that would keep away all harm including evil spirits, a robe on which she painted a dream that hid him from the sight of everyone and everything, a magical spear that could pierce anything, a magical shield that would ward off everything and a magical club that would break anything. She stitched mountains onto the sides of his moccasins so that he could leap from hill to hill without touching the valleys and blue beaded dragonflies so that he could escape all danger.'

'I get it,' said Grace. 'You can never catch a dragonfly.'

Uncle smiled.

'On his deerskin leggings she stitched wolf tracks so that he would never get tired no matter how long he travelled. On his shirt she painted a tepee circle so he would have shelter wherever he went.'

'Do fathers take care of their children like mothers do?' I asked.

'You're so dumb, Bruce,' Grace answered. 'Your father showed me how to catch worms.'

'When the boy was older, one summer the land lost all its fertility. Nothing grew. There wasn't even pickerelweed to eat. Stone Boy's tribe was starving. Buffalo attack when people are vulnerable and the buffalo chose to stampede through his tribe's settlement and destroy everything and everyone.'

'Buffalo don't attack people. People attack buffalo,' I said firmly. 'That's why there aren't any buffalo anymore.'

'Out West, Indians genuinely were afraid of buffalo. When they stampede they kill. Stone Boy heard their thundering hooves and knew what was happening. So in his magical moccasins he strode towards his family's village warding the buffalo off with his magical shield. Wearing his magical cloak so they could not see him he stood in front of the village and with his massive weight of heavy stone he stepped on the chest of every single buffalo and their breath rushed out of their mouths and nostrils. It rushed out with such force it became a mighty whirling, twisting wind that broke trees, tore up the grass, threw water from the lakes and piled up rocks and earth.

'The buffalo in their dying breath caused such an upheaval and renewal of the land that it become fertile once more. His tribe, including his two older sisters, were grateful and now they loved him even though they hadn't wanted him in the first place.'

'You're telling me I should be happy 'cause my mum's pregnant. What if she has another girl?' Grace asked.

'Then I'll tell you another true story about a girl baby.'

That evening, as we had been promised, the young children – me, Perry and Grace – were allowed to sleep in the tent overnight for the first time. The days were getting shorter and by the time we had changed into our pyjamas in the cottage and taken our sleeping bags and pillows out to the tent it was almost dark.

'Keep it zipped shut,' Grace commanded us. 'I don't want any mosquitoes getting in. If you want to go back to the cottage you have to ask me first.'

The three of us laid our sleeping bags side by side, with our heads nearest the entrance and with Grace in the middle. In our dark cocoon we listened to the utter silence of the night and it was only a moment before I realised the night wasn't silent at all but filled with all sorts of noises I didn't hear when I slept in my own bed. I felt safe and scared both at the same time. I asked, 'What's that?' each time I heard an unfamiliar sound.

'It's an evil spirit coming to get us,' Grace replied on one occasion. Perry told her to shut up and go to sleep.

Grace and Perry did fall asleep but I didn't. I was too excited about sleeping outside and once I was sure they wouldn't hear me I quietly unzipped the tent flap, pulled my sleeping bag outside onto the grass, crawled back into it and with it tucked tightly around my neck I watched the sky for shooting stars. Beyond the North Star, the northern lights danced their green undulations on the horizon.

'What are you doing?' Grace whispered. I hadn't heard her creep out of the tent.

'I'm watching stars fall from the sky,' I answered.

She reached back into the tent and dragged out her sleeping bag, which she put beside mine.

'Move over,' she commanded and instead of getting in her sleeping bag she crawled into mine. We lay there not talking, not even whispering, both looking at the Milky Way and watching for shooting stars. Grace fell asleep quite quickly. The warmth of her beside me made me feel snug and restful but I took longer to fall asleep.

Next morning, I woke up first, to the pink glow of dawn and the familiar sounds of a new summer day. It had cooled overnight and the ground and sleeping bags were wet with dew. I lay there for a while, perfectly still, watching dewdrops drip from the willow leaves, like tiny fairies parachuting into the grass. The air was filled with freshness. No one was up yet, not Grace, not Perry, not anyone. I slid out of the sleeping bag and in my pyjamas went for a walk, leaving a trail of footsteps over the soft wet grass, onto the cold gravel road, up to the top of the hill where through the line of white pine trees on the road I could see the orange sun, just breaking the horizon. There was no wind at all, and I felt as calm as candy floss. When I got back to the cottage Grace had rolled up both our sleeping bags. Perry was still asleep.

'I'm going to tell my parents that you should come camping the next time we go,' she said. She kissed me on my cheek and headed home for breakfast.

TRAINING
POPEYE

There were animals in the city – robins, raccoons – but they seemed anonymous. At the cottage you got to know them as individuals. You watched the muskrat leave the boathouse, go fishing and come back home. You watched the mallard make its nest and raise its ducklings. You saw where fish spawned or where kingfishers lived. The way Uncle Reub put it, 'Like us they all earn a living.'

'Who started that screeching?' I thought.

I always got up before anyone else but one morning the gulls started their squawking just before dawn. 'They're getting ready for war,' I imagined, and I went straight outside in my pyjamas to see what was happening. But as suddenly as they had started shrieking they stopped and now the birds were perfectly quiet, floating peacefully on the lake.

'They're pretending they like each other,' I decided, and went back inside to make breakfast.

I poured myself a glass of milk, toasted a bagel, buttered it and sprinkled it with cinnamon sugar. I always saved bread crusts in a large glass jar when I did the clearing up after meals, and I took several small pieces of crust, went outside and looked for Popeye. The sun had broken through the trees. It was perfectly calm and indescribably beautiful.

I whistled. Uncle had taught me how and my whistle was much louder than Rob's. I didn't really expect Popeye to come to me but from all the gulls floating on the lake, just one took to the air and glided to a landing on the shore where it stared straight at me. Even though it looked just like all the other herring gulls I knew it was Popeye.

I sat in my uncle's favourite lawn chair, rested my plate on my lap and threw a bread crust into the lush green, deep and dewy grass. I'd fed Popeye like that before, when Popeye landed on the dock. I would walk towards the dock in a measured and deliberate way, as if life was in slow motion, then with an unhurried underhand throw, toss a crust towards the bird. I always turned and looked away but out of the corner of my eye would see Popeye walk over to the crust, pick it up and fly off to the lake where he wetted it and swallowed it. I thought I was quite clever to train the bird – such a wild thing. Now, on the grass and much closer to me than the bird ever was on the dock, Popeye waddled over on his enormous pink gull feet, grabbed the crust and flew back to the lake where he ate it.

I ate my crunchy breakfast and soon Popeye was back, standing once more on the sandy shore, looking straight at me. Just staring. I threw him another crust and again Popeye lifted himself off the shoreline, flew over but instead of landing on the grass he continued straight to me and then suddenly I felt an enormous weight on my head. I had never felt anything so heavy in my whole life, ever, and was almost overcome by excitement. I stayed perfectly still, feeling the huge webbed feet trying to get a purchase, wondering what would happen next. I kept silent and still. I had an impulse to reach up and clutch the bird's silken white body, but before I could Popeye's big yellow bill was right in front of my eyes. There was a red spot on the bottom bill I had never noticed before. Popeye grabbed the remaining bagel from the plate and flew off to the lake with it, taking off with such ease that I felt only lightness.

For the next week I got up extra early each morning, toasted a bagel and went out hoping to experience the joy I felt once more. I tried spreading strawberry jam, peanut butter, cream cheese and honey on my breakfast but the gulls languidly floated in the lake. If Popeye was amongst them he didn't let on to me that he was. I wondered what I had done to upset the bird.

Then one late morning, as the sun wandered towards noon, he was back, standing on the dock, looking like he was hungry. Steven and Perry were visiting. It was now late summer but the air was still hanging with heat and while I went into the cottage to toast a bagel, the boys decided they would all go for a swim. Sometimes we waded into the lake from the shore, sometimes we rowed out to the raft and swam there and sometimes we did what they did today, ran down the dock and belly flopped into the shallow water.

Steve was first. He ran down the dock and as he did so Popeye gently lifted himself into the air while Steve did a perfect belly flop. Perry raced after his brother and almost landed on top of him, landing on the lake like a seaplane.

'That hurt,' he screamed with a smile.

When I returned Popeye was floating on the water beside the dock and Rob was racing as fast as he could across the lawn, down the dock and into the air, launching himself onto the water with his arms out like wings.

'I hit the bottom!' he said to no one in particular when he stood up, and the lake water running down his face was pink and he was holding the top of his head.

I ran back inside the cottage.

'Uncle Reub, you'd better come,' I said and by the time my uncle and my mother were outside, Rob, Steve and Perry had left the lake and Rob was holding a towel over his head.

Uncle examined Rob's head then told him to keep the towel tight on it, then talked quietly to Mum.

'Bruce, tell Grace's mother there's been an accident and she's going to drive us to Civic Hospital,' Mum told me.

When they returned several hours later, Robert looked embarrassed, with a face mask over the top of his head. It was tied under his chin.

The following day, Uncle Reub examined Robert's shaved patch under the face mask.

'I don't like the way they clamped it,' I heard my uncle say. 'There should be a drain. There's sand in that serum. We'd better go to Mount Sinai and have this done properly.'

Mum was not herself all day. She walked up to Mrs Nichols' and telephoned Dad. She drove over to Cedar Bay with Grace's mother and arranged that I would stay with Steven and Perry. She made lunch for Robert but forgot to do so for me or my uncle or herself.

In the afternoon Dad arrived and drove me to Cedar Bay.

'Do what you're told,' Mum told me before we left. 'Don't go off daydreaming like you do. They'll worry about you. We'll be back on Saturday.' And she gave me a kiss and a tight squeeze that almost hurt.

'Do what you're told,' Dad said as he left.

My parents, brother and Angus left for the city that afternoon and for the next three days I lived at Steve and Perry's and was unhappy. I wasn't unhappy because my parents were away or because Rob had hurt himself or because I was staying with Perry. I was unhappy because I wanted Popeye to land on my head again.

Perry's mother made delicious breakfasts. Eggs sunny side up with crispy bacon and toasted Wonder Bread. Mum never fried bacon and told me that white sliced bread had no goodness in it.

I told my friends I couldn't stay at Grace's because I was a boy. Steve said it was Grace's father's decision. Her mother didn't mind.

Steve wouldn't go to the fort with Perry and me although he did go swimming when we did. On the second day, on our way to the fort, we found a raccoon sitting beside a shallow pond in the woods. It didn't run away and as we cautiously and quietly approached it we saw it fall over on its side.

'It's sick,' Perry said.

'It needs a vet,' I replied.

We watched the raccoon's eyes close and open and then it fell on its side once more and it had to use all its strength to sit up again.

I was the first to touch it, gently and tentatively on the top of its neck, then with a little more firmness on the top of its head, then on its body. The animal offered no resistance or resentment.

We were on our haunches on both sides of the raccoon when I said, 'We'll take it to Dr Sweeting.' I put my left hand under the animal's chest and my right hand under its rump and needed all my strength to stand up with it.

The only way I was strong enough to carry the sick raccoon was by holding it tight against my chest, leaning back. Even so I had to hand the heavy animal to Perry and we passed it back and forth many times until we emerged from the woods and walked down the point to Dr Sweeting's.

Mrs Sweeting looked alarmed when she answered the door and Dr Sweeting was angry and annoyed when he saw us with the sick animal.

'Boys, take it over there and put it down,' he said, pointing towards his tool shed.

Dr Sweeting went into the shed, put on overalls then walked over to the raccoon and told us to go back to the cottage veranda.

When we were there, he put leather gardening gloves on his hands then with the blade of the shovel smashed it with such force on the raccoon's head that we heard the animal's skull crack open like a hard-boiled egg.

'You can come back now,' he said.

I didn't move. The animal had needed help. It was beautiful. It was soft. It hadn't harmed anyone. And Dr Sweeting killed it.

'Doctors are supposed to make things better!' I screamed at the man. 'My uncle says you take an oath to make everyone better!' I fought to look straight at Dr Sweeting without blinking but my tears wouldn't let me.

Dr Sweeting looked sternly at us. 'Don't you ever touch an animal like that again, you hear? They're goddam dangerous. Don't you know that coon had rabies? It might be the one that gave rabies to the Nichols' milking cow. Now go into the house and Mrs Sweeting will give the two of you a good scrub!'

Somehow, seeing that innocent animal die made me more anxious than ever to see Popeye once more. Everything about that bird was perfect. His feet were as pink and clean as a little baby. His feathers were as grey as my father's best wool suit, as black as a moonless sky, as white as early morning clouds. His beak was yellow like the sun, his red spot as shiny bright as a traffic light. That bird was summer itself.

On Saturday, Dad arrived with flowers and a cake for Steve and Perry's parents and silently drove me back to our cottage.

'What did they do to you?' I asked my brother when I saw him but all Rob said was, 'I hate hospitals!' and I knew not to ask any more. 'I'm not allowed in the lake for two weeks,' he continued.

I walked to the front lawn but there were no gulls anywhere. For the next three days the lake was rough and the rain relentless. My family went to see a movie at Mr Yudin's theatre in Peterborough on one day, over to Steve and Perry's on another. On the fourth day I knew before I got out of bed that the sun had returned. The air was fresher when I went outside. A cormorant was paddling past the cottage, only its black head and the top of its long neck visible in the water. Off shore there were at least a hundred gulls, too far away to see easily.

And then I saw it. Amongst the foot deep seaweed the wind had dumped on the shore was Popeye's wing. I felt a shiver start in my jaws, move to my shoulders then down my back. I tore seaweed away, strand by strand, revealing the gull's plump body and finally its head. There was fishing line going into the bird's beak. The line was knotted in the seaweed and I dug it all out. It was twice as long as the dock. Then I noticed. There was no red dot on the lower beak. It wasn't Popeye, and I felt like dancing.

Now I wanted to know why the gull had a fishing line in its mouth. I finished separating the bird from its seaweed wrapping, washed it off in the lake, took it from the shore, placed it under the tree house and went to the bunkhouse to get my uncle.

'There's a seagull that died and I want to know why. It's not Popeye,' I shouted to my uncle through the bunkhouse screen door. 'Bring your things. It's under the tree house.'

Angus was sniffing the bird when I returned to it and soon we were joined by my uncle, still in his striped pyjamas.

'Let's move into the sunshine,' he said. 'It's warmer there.'

I carried the solid bird to the middle of the front lawn.

'It's not Popeye,' I said again.

'You can tell?' Uncle asked.

'Popeye had a red spot on his beak chin. This seagull doesn't.'

'Why is it important to you it's not Popeye?' Uncle asked as he tugged on the fishing line coming from its beak.

'Because Popeye's my friend and this is any old seagull,' I answered.

'So we should be sad if one gull dies but not another?' he asked.

'Yes, because I fed Popeye and he once landed on my head,' I replied.

'I understand. You made a connection with Popeye, and if he was so relaxed he was willing to stand on your head, I think he also made a connection with you. There's a lesson there, Brucie. You see the world a different way when you make connections. Now then, I think we can ascertain the cause of death without needing to do a post-mortem. This bird is heavy so it hasn't starved to death. It swallowed a fishing hook so it died from an infection caused by the hook.'

'How can you tell?' I asked.

'That's what happens without penicillin.'

'Shouldn't it know not to eat fishing hooks?' I asked.

'I'm sure it did know not to eat hooks, but it didn't know it was eating one. It thought it was eating a frog or a minnow. Looks like the gull took a fisherman's bait by mistake and the fisherman cut his line when he saw what happened.'

'But that's not fair,' I continued. 'The bird didn't do anything wrong. If God decides each year who lives and who dies, why did he decide the seagull should die now the way it did?'

Uncle answered, 'Bruce, I simply don't know why. Perhaps one day I will but I agree with you, how can a benevolent God, a good God, do such things to innocent creatures?'

'If you're a grown-up and you don't believe in God then why should I?' I asked and my uncle said, 'Bruce, I'll tell you something I've never told anyone else. In 1929, three years after I graduated in medicine, I was working at the Mayo Clinic in Minnesota. I developed a new way to remove tonsils from children, a safer way. That method saved hundreds, maybe thousands of lives. I was front-page news all over the United States and Canada. Then my mother, your grandmother, pricked her finger on a darning needle while repairing a hole in one of my father's socks, and two weeks later she died in front of me. I was this famous young doctor and there was nothing I could do to save her. That's when I stopped believing in God.'

'But you're still religious. You say the prayer over wine on Friday.'

'Yes, but that's not the same as believing in God. That's respect for our traditions. I say the prayer because your mother feels better when I do. I've never told her I don't believe in an intervening God. But I tell you this, Bruce. When I look at the beauty of the natural world I can't help but think that once upon a time there was a benevolent force – call it God if you like – that created such splendour. Even the inside of that seagull is exquisite in its perfection although I can't say I'm much good at bird anatomy. Or sewing them up afterwards.'

'OK then. You don't need to cut it open,' I said, and carried the bird to the back of the cottage, beyond the vegetable patch and buried it there. As I dug the soft earth I wondered whether the fisherman who killed the seagull was sad. Or even that he knew it died. You're not sad when you kill fish because you eat them. But no one kills seagulls to eat. I wondered why I was so upset when Dr Sweeting killed the raccoon and decided I was troubled by the cruel way he killed it. Then I thought maybe it's better to die fast a cruel way, than to die slow the way the seagull must have. Then I thought it must be lunchtime and wondered whether Dad brought fresh bagels back with him from Toronto.

Popeye returned a few days later and took crusts that I gave him, but never landed on my head again.

ADULTS'
PARTIES

Every summer weekend the adults danced. Sometimes they went to The Pines in Bridgenorth on Saturday night, for a square dance or a round dance with a live band, but more often they gathered in one cottage or another, played their own music and sang their own songs. The mothers always organised the parties and got food ready but the fathers played all the instruments. I didn't know why. That's just how it was.

One Saturday the party was at my cottage so my mother had lots to do. She told Robert to clean out the stone fireplace on the front lawn and pile firewood beside it. He didn't want to but he did. She told my father to go to the butchers on George Street and get twelve T-bone steaks. 'If they don't have enough, get sirloins,' she shouted as he left. 'And don't forget the corn.'

She told me to get Grace and go to Mrs Nichols' to collect twenty-four butter tarts and two peach pies. She handed me a ten dollar bill and said, 'Don't take any change from Mrs Nichols. If you do I'll be cross with you. You and Grace can each have a butter tart.' After I left she busied herself in the kitchen, making coleslaw. Grace's mother was bringing fresh dill pickles.

I put a leash on Angus – we'd be crossing the highway and I needed something to tie him up with on Mrs Nichols' veranda – and found Grace down on her dock fishing, and we all walked together up the hill to Mrs Nichols' farmhouse. We enjoyed going there. Mrs Nichols had grey hair and was really old but there was something about her that made us feel good.

Grace knocked firmly on the screen door while I tied Angus's leash to a rocking chair.

'Children, you're early,' Mrs Nichols said. 'Come,' and we followed her through the hallway into the large kitchen at the back. The whole house, even the outside veranda, smelled like a delicious bakery and on the kitchen table were the peach pies and butter tarts.

'Your mama told me you'd be picking up the baking,' she said. 'I've got something for you. Sit,' and from a cream-coloured pitcher she poured each of us a glass of milk and gave us gingerbread men dressed in bathing suits. 'Them's you,' she said, her eyes beaming.

I saw happiness in her eyes. I wanted to tell her I didn't like gingerbread but knew that I shouldn't, so I said, 'Thank you. May I please take it home to show my mother?' and she replied, 'Yes.'

Everyone knew that Mrs Nichols' peach pies were tastier than anything store bought, even tastier than anything bought from the bakery and on this visit Grace asked how she made them. Her recipe was simple. The crust was no more than flour, shortening, water and salt. The peaches were freestones from Niagara and her secret was that she never cooked them. Her other secret was her glaze. She made it from corn starch with a little squeezed peach juice and a few drops of vanilla. She always poured her glaze into the crust first then as it set pressed the peach slices into it until they were covered. Her pies looked as good as they tasted. Mrs Nichols' peach pie with fresh vanilla ice cream from the local dairy was my favourite dessert in the whole world.

After Grace had eaten her gingerbread man and we both finished our milk, I gave Mrs Nichols the ten dollar bill I had in my bathing suit pocket. She got her purse and gave me two dollars change. I explained to her that Mum told me she would be angry if I came back with change and she put the dollar bills back in her purse.

'Don't wait 'til your mother sends you,' she said as we left. 'I make candy,' and she waved a goodbye.

I carried the two pies in their glass Pyrex dishes and Grace carried the box of butter tarts and on the hill down to the cottages we sat down to eat the tarts we were promised. Angus wanted some but I didn't give him any.

'Your mother wouldn't know if she gave you change. We'd each have a dollar,' Grace said.

I thought about that for a while. I got an allowance, fifty cents a week, but I'd like to get a dollar. That's what Rob got.

'I think Mrs Nichols needs the money. The butter tarts are melting,' I replied and Grace left it at that. When we returned to the cottage Mum gave each of us a quarter.

That evening Rob and I had sandwiches and coleslaw for supper and although we asked to stay up for the party we weren't allowed to, and as darkness arrived we went to our bedrooms and bed.

At night, when the lights first go out, in the pitch black I saw nothing at all but then, ever so gradually, the room as always seemed to get lighter and soon I could see the walls, the dresser, even moths clinging to the white tiles on the ceiling. Moonlight shone through the curtains and the cowboys on their horses on the curtains seemed to move and the desert glisten. In early spring, when I visited the cottage with Dad, it was so cold getting into bed I pulled three blankets onto myself and, when I was still cold, the rag rug from the floor, until I fell asleep in my own warmth. Now in late summer, although nights should be fresh it was sultry, and I threw the blanket off and listened to the grown-ups through the thin plywood wall that separated my bedroom from where they all were.

I tried to stay awake and listen to everything. At the last party in July I had to go to the bathroom and on my way back I'd peeked out and everyone was dancing close together and smoking at the same time. Only the oil lamps were burning. The bright electric lights on the ceiling and the two on the wall had been turned off. Uncle was in the corner, an oil lamp on the table beside him, a smile on his face, his bald head shining like a full moon, reading some book or other.

'Food's almost ready.' It was my father's voice, and soon after that the giggling and shouting got softer and I fell asleep. I was awakened by a mighty clash. The music was thumping and the floor of the cottage actually bouncing and I wanted to know exactly what that clash was so I went to the bathroom and on my way back, opened the hall door a little and looked out. Angus was curious too. He got out of his basket in the clothes cupboard and also came to the hall door. Mr Yudin had two tin garbage can lids and was clashing them together. I recognised everything else, Dr Sweeting's bass that he made from an aluminium washing basin, a broom handle and a rope, Grace's father playing the clarinet, my dad playing the fiddle with Mum watching him, smiling, Perry's father playing piano. And there was my uncle, playing the ukulele.

I smiled at that, Uncle Reub joining in the music. Angus stayed by the door but I went back to bed and the smell of steaks and rye and cigarette smoke followed me. I lay on my bed and recognised Dr Sweeting's voice when he sang 'Is You Is or Is You Ain't My Baby'. Then Mum sang 'Paper Moon' and everyone went quiet. Perry's mother sang 'Dancing Cheek to Cheek' and when Perry's father sang 'Walking My Baby Back Home' everyone joined in. They all sang 'Hava Nagila' together, faster and faster, laughing loud when they finished.

'Reub, your turn,' I heard my mother say and I heard my uncle's high, gentle voice. All the other voices gradually fell away and through my father's gentle violin I could hear my uncle sing.

When I remember every little thing you used to do
I'm so lonely!
Ev'ry road I walk along I've walked along with you.
No wonder I am lonely!
The sky is blue,
The night is cold.
The moon is new
But love is old.
And while I'm waiting here
This heart of mine is singing:
'Lover, come back to me!'

The next morning I watched the new day arrive as I always did, gradually, first with a little light through the curtains, just enough for me to see the cowboys on their horses, then brighter light between the curtains. That told me it was time to draw them open and look for the birds that were singing, but that I never saw. Each summer day's arrival was that peaceful. It was always a good way to decide what to do that day.

I got out of bed very carefully because I knew which floorboards were squeaky and which ones weren't and I didn't want to wake anyone up. I got dressed and went into the main room of the cottage. Angus vacuumed the floor for party leftovers. When I looked at the number of cigarette butts in the ashtrays I thought that the party must have got bigger after I fell asleep for the night. Quietly I collected the ashtrays and glasses and dessert dishes and took them to the kitchen. I went back and puffed up the cushions on the sofa and put the chairs back around the dining room table. When I returned to the kitchen Uncle Reub was there, in his dark trousers and his new coloured shirt.

'I'll wash. You dry,' he whispered.

When Mum got up a few hours later she gave me such a hard squeeze I thought I'd never breathe again.

THE NEW BOAT

I didn't understand why my father was so restless that morning but later that day I just smiled and smiled. After helping Reg Muskratt salvage the abandoned boat on Kelly's Island, Dad couldn't get it out of his mind. Quite simply he had to have it, more than anything else he could think of.

Mum didn't know what Dad had done but the previous Friday he'd left work early and instead of driving straight from the city to the cottage he drove past it, up to the Mud Lake Reserve where he met with Mr Muskratt and made a deal – a good deal for both of them. Mr Muskratt would haul the boat out of the water and sand and repaint the red keel. Then Dad would buy the freshly painted boat from him for cash and for our own fourteen footer with its Evinrude motor, a more practical boat for Mr Muskratt to go fishing in.

This morning, Dad had left the cottage just after dawn, picked up a brand-new Johnson forty-horsepower motor he'd ordered from the Bridgenorth marina, put it in the back of his station wagon and taken it up to Mud Lake, all before 9 a.m.

When he got back to the cottage, he pretended that nothing much was happening although Mum and I and Uncle Reub knew that something or other was cooking. We could tell by Dad's earnestness and urgency but we asked nothing, even when he said, as soon as he got back, that he was going fishing. After he left in the boat the grown-ups gossiped with each other trying to figure out what he was up to.

By the time he'd boated back up to the Reserve, Mr Muskratt and young James Coppaway had hung the new motor from the boat's transom, attached the battery and the steering cables and had taken it out for a quick spin to make sure everything worked well. I knew that before he left the Reserve my father would have shaken hands with everyone who helped get the boat ready, doing his short bow that he always did when he shook someone's hand. I was first to see the boat arriving and called everyone else. My father seemed happier than I had ever seen him – joyous really – when everyone found the new boat as beautiful as he and I did.

Dad had a new assistant at the flower store and stayed at the cottage all that week. He sanded and revarnished the boat's inner cedar hull, the mahogany bow and rear decks and the maple dashboard. He installed a removable canopy, a chrome compass on the dashboard, two chrome rearview mirrors, a chrome port and starboard light with a flag staff in the middle for the bow deck, another chrome flag staff at the back and two more chrome port and starboard lights. He bought foam-rubber filled, white, waterproof seats and made two licence plates, 32E12637, from aluminium letters mounted on varnished cedar plaques and used copper nails to mount the plaques on both sides of the bow. Dad told us that when we went to the powwow Mr Whetung had organised on the Mud Lake Reserve for late August, we would go by boat no matter what the weather was like.

*

On the day of the powwow, Lake Chemong was as smooth as oilcloth and my parents decided it would be a perfect day for a longer boat trip, to go blueberry picking and have a picnic up at the Buckhorn lock first, then return to the Reserve for the powwow.

I was as proud as my dad was of our new boat. The powerful engine roared like a lion but even so it was amazingly quiet compared to the old Evinrude. Uncle Reub decided to take along a length of rubber hosepipe and he used that to talk to anyone else in the boat as we cruised up the lake. At first, my father travelled very slowly close to shore, waving to any cottagers he saw on Long Point, then on Cedar Bay, then on Poplar Point. After that he accelerated out into the lake, raced past Kelly's Island then through Harrington Narrows and into Buckhorn Lake. The boat sliced through the waters as if it was travelling on a velvet ribbon. For the final seven miles through Buckhorn Lake everyone sat quiet as we soaked in the beauty of the empty islands and lakeshore they raced by.

At Buckhorn we docked by the lock, took the apple baskets we brought with us, walked past the lock and the red-rocked rapids, crossed the highway and were in a landscape that to me was foreign and exciting, like a completely different country, all sparkling pink granite, white and green mosses, birch and pine trees. Blueberry country. The sun inched high in the sky and the cumulus clouds were whiter than cotton batting.

'It's really difficult, picking blueberries,' I said to my uncle, as we both stood still and stared intently at the ground around us. 'Picking raspberries is easy. Even the black ones are easy to see. You really have to look hard to see blueberries here. This is more serious than picking raspberries.'

We took short steps, both of us with our bodies bent over, scanning the mosses and twigs and fallen leaves we were walking through.

'Brucie, it's how your mind works. You train it. When you walk somewhere you think your mind takes in everything, but really, it doesn't. It only takes in part of it. It sees the big picture, the sky, the trees, the shrubs, the vegetation, the rocks. But when you're berry picking your mind sees none of that. Your mind's eye only sees blueberries until your real eyes see them.'

In the sun-dappled rocky landscape, my eyes were the first to see there was a carpet of blueberries under my feet. They were everywhere, thousands of them, tens of thousands, millions, all waiting to be individually picked. It took less than an hour for my family to fill all our four-pint apple baskets.

Mum had come prepared. Back at the boat she set out our picnic on a lock-side table – cheese, lettuce and sweet dill pickle sandwiches, Kool-Aid from the thermos and, for dessert, cream she had brought along especially to pour on the fresh berries. Each time any other boaters looked at my new boat I worried whether they would come over and say, 'I had a boat just like that but I lost it.' We enjoyed our picnic so much we almost missed the powwow.

THE POWWOW

On visits to Mud Lake Mrs Whetung had told us that where we were, on the tip of the peninsula between Chemong and Buckhorn, was the only land anywhere around that still belonged to the Indians. I enjoyed my visits. The men didn't say much, which made them mysterious. The women were different. To me, Mrs Knott and Mrs Muskratt and Mrs Whetung and Mrs Jacobs, they all seemed warm and motherly and talkative.

Grace's mother told us it was the Whetung family's idea to start an annual powwow as a way to get the locals and the summer people to visit. Mrs Whetung had a gift shop in her living room. There was no hydro at Mud Lake, no telephones either, so news about the powwow was spread up and down the lake by word of mouth. I had seen a notice in the Bridgenorth general store.

By the time my family and I got back to Mud Lake we could hear the powwow taking place. Dad docked our new boat beside Grace's father's sleek inboard and we ran to the Reserve's baseball diamond where the men on the Reserve had set up a totem pole on the pitcher's mound. Mr Muskratt, Mr Whetung, Mr Boudreault and Mr Taylor, all wearing big feather headdresses and buckskin shirts and trousers, were dancing around it while Mr Coppaway and his sons beat tom-toms. I thought they looked slightly embarrassed. The women also wore beaded buckskin and had feathers in their hair and they looked a whole lot happier than their menfolk. They were all rhythmically stamping their feet on the baseball diamond's dry earth, beckoning everyone to join in.

I moved over to stand beside Grace, whose mother had put a feather in her hair and was stamping her feet and using her hand on her mouth to make whooping sounds. I thought she looked breathtakingly beautiful and ridiculous both at the same time. Using a megaphone Mr Whetung, who was Master of Ceremonies, invited everyone to join hands, make a circle and participate in their last dance. Uncle Reub had been sitting cross-legged on the ground near second base but he got up and joined the circle, holding hands with Mrs Muskratt and Dr Sweeting's wife. I joined hands with Grace and her mother. The drummers began their metric beating and most of the people in the circle started stamping their feet, but I didn't. It didn't feel right to me.

'Dance!' Grace commanded, and because she told me to I did, and I continued to stamp my feet even after the drums stopped.

After that everyone politely applauded and we broke up into small groups. Reg Muskratt, Mr Coppaway and his two sons went off with my father and me to inspect the boat. I wished I had my dad's movie camera when all five men, four Indians in feathered headdresses and my dad in a red-checked shirt and work trousers, all got in the boat and examined the improvements. Mum joined Mrs Whetung and Mrs Boudreault who were going to explain how they use local plants and tell of their tribe's history. Uncle Reub talked with Mrs Muskratt. When he returned to the boat he had a brown paper bag of roots he had bought from her.

'Mrs Muskratt collected these sweet flag roots right over there,' he told me, pointing to the black, mucky ground beside the dock where sweet flag almost as tall as he was, was growing. 'We can get more if we need to from frog bog.'

'What's it for?' I asked, and my uncle explained that Mrs Muskratt told him that sweet flag tea, made from those roots, was good for a sore throat and that some of the singers at the powwow kept pieces in their mouths to keep their voices clear.

'That was most interesting,' Mum said when she returned to the dock.

'They think braided sweetgrass is the hair of mother earth and it protects you from evil spirits. It gets that vanilla smell only after it's hung and dried. The tobacco they grow by the baseball diamond – they say it's a purifier and represents the south. Sweetgrass represents the north. Do you know they didn't have a lawyer when they signed the treaty for this reserve?'

'That was long ago,' Dad said.

'No it wasn't. It's not much more than twenty-five years ago.'

She bent down and untied the bowline.

'Reub, you know Indian history. Sit with me in the boat,' she said.

As she got in she turned to her brother, and said, 'I don't think we treated these people well.'

They got in the boat and even at full speed it seemed to take longer to get home than it did to go all the way to Buckhorn that morning. Rob fell asleep. Mum and Uncle Reub talked.

After we docked, my father turned the boat around so that the bow faced the lake. The air was freshening and he didn't want waves to wash over the flat transom.

'Brucie, let's go in the tent,' Uncle suggested, and while the rest of the family went in the cottage the two of us crawled into our hideaway.

'Your mother was upset today when she learned how we took the Indians' land. Mrs Whetung told her the government had three lawyers at the treaty meeting but none of them kept minutes so there's no way of knowing what was said. On the other hand, I had a very interesting day. Mr Muskratt's wife, Mrs Muskratt, she's a wise woman.'

'Grace's mother says she wears the pants in their family,' I replied and my uncle smiled at that.

'She means she's as perceptive as your mother is. Mrs Muskratt told me that wapato tubers were good to eat if they were baked over an open fire, and that yellow pond-lily rootstocks could be ground into flour and so could water lily seeds.

'She asked me what I did for a living and I explained I was an eye, ear, nose and throat doctor but I was also what Edgar Ten Fingers called a "right man". She asked me where I used my knowledge and I told her I wasn't using it. You know what she said? She told me I was a fool.'

As he spoke, Uncle Reub took a crooked sweet flag root from the brown paper bag, cut off a piece with his pocket knife, put it in his mouth and started chewing it.

'The Oglala Sioux crush sweet flag roots and make tea from

it and they give the tea to their puppies so they grow up to be brave watchdogs.'

Uncle continued chewing the piece of root until it turned to paste, then he dribbled it from his mouth into his cupped left hand, something that I thought a grown-up shouldn't do.

'Sioux braves use it too,' he continued. 'They chew the roots to make a paste then they rub their faces with it. It prevents fear or excitement when they face an enemy.

'Brucie, Mrs Muskratt isn't the first person to call me a fool. Your mother's also called me a fool and I paid no attention to her. Have you heard her say, "If one person calls you a jackass, pay no attention. If two people call you a jackass, it's time to get a saddle"? Well it's time I got a saddle.'

I watched, perplexed. I didn't know what my uncle meant by saying it was time to get a saddle but I was more astonished by what he was doing, smearing his soft, round cheeks with chewed sweet flag root. He looked like a baby that was sloppy with his cereal.

'Uncle Reub, who's your enemy?' I eventually asked.

'Bruce, you're younger than your brother but you're a wise boy and if you don't understand now, you will when you grow up. Most people think that others are their enemies but they're wrong. Your biggest enemy can be yourself. It's time I faced that.'

'Are you going to wash that off before we go inside?' I asked.

'Yes, of course I will,' Uncle replied. 'We don't want them to think I'm off my rocker.'

He continued, 'Do you know where I left that skunk tail? I can tie it to my foot then I'll be like a skunk and not run away.'

As we walked from the tent to the cottage I asked my uncle one more question.

'When do I have to grow up?' I asked, and Uncle Reub smiled and put his arm around my shoulder. 'Robert and the other boys would probably ask, "When can I be a grown-up?" Your question is better and it's for you to decide. When I feel good, and I do feel good right now, I hope I never have to.'

THE
AGRICULTURAL
FAIR

I was eating raspberries in the vegetable patch when I heard a car coming down the point. I knew it wasn't the milkman or the bread man or Mr Everett collecting garbage. It didn't sound like any of their trucks. Fathers didn't arrive until Friday so it wasn't any of them. When I saw a taxicab I stopped eating raspberries and stared at it. Taxicabs shouldn't visit cottages. It was wrong. They were for city people. In cities.

The dusty brown taxicab slowly rumbled past the other cottages and stopped at mine. As the driver opened the car door Uncle Reub stepped out of the bunkhouse.

'Good morning. You found us. We'll be ready in five minutes.'

'Morning, sir. Fine day. Your instructions were right on the trigger.'

With a smile on his face that made him look like the man in the moon, Uncle Reub turned to me and said, 'You and I are going to the Peterborough Ex. Just you and me. Go in and put on a shirt and some shoes. I'll meet you here.'

'Uncle must have gone to Mrs Nichols to use her phone,' I thought as I laced up my shoes. I put on my favourite cowboy shirt, and as I left Mum kissed me and said, 'Look after each other.'

Uncle Reub, wearing the shirt he bought at the Bridgenorth General Store, stood beside the taxicab and opened the side door as I approached then followed me in. 'Everyone on the point is going on Saturday. It will be better today. Just farmers.'

I felt extra special, riding in the back of the taxicab. I never went anywhere in a taxicab, even in the city. It was either buses or the new subway or my mother drove. Both of us silently looked out of our windows as we drove towards town. I knew every bit of the road from the cottage to Bridgenorth but once past that hamlet, even though I visited the town almost every week, I still felt like I was travelling in a foreign land.

'Mr Gilchrist will have his best stock at the fair,' Uncle said, as we passed a barn on which was written in large white letters 'GILCHRIST FARM'.

'Brucie, do you know there's a red ribbon to be won for the cow with the best udder? From what you told me about Mrs Blewett, I think her husband might enter her in the competition?'

We giggled ourselves silly at that thought.

The taxicab driver drove us straight down George Street, past the new City Hall, Eaton's, Woolworths, Mr Yudin's theatre, Fosters' Restaurant and Canadian Tire, then past the municipal wharf on Little Lake and on to the fairgrounds at the southern end of town where he let us off at the main gate. I was surprised to see that Mrs Nichols was in the ticket booth.

'Well, it's so very good to see you here today, young man,' she said as we reached the booth. 'I do this for the Agricultural Society,' she continued, addressing my uncle who bought two tickets from her.

'Don't forget to visit the home-baking tent,' she called as we left.

'In Mandan we have cow wrestling and bucking broncos at the agricultural show,' Uncle said.

'What's that got to do with the Ex?' I asked.

'Nothing. I just thought you might be interested in what happens at other fairs. Tell you what. We don't have pig races in Mandan but they do here. Shall we see?' Uncle asked.

'Yes please,' I replied, and we started towards the racetrack but stopped to join the crowd listening to the music coming from the bandstand.

The Peterborough Civic Concert Band – all men in red blazers – was playing 'It's a Long Way to Tipperary'.

'They play it like a marching song,' Uncle confided to me. 'That's because during the war they were a regiment band, a marching band. It's really a love song.'

'Mum and Grace's mother sing love songs but they don't sound like this,' I replied.

'Makes you want to dance, eh?' Uncle replied and he raised his hands in the air and lightly turned in a tight circle on the toes of his feet.

'The love is in the words, Brucie. Paddy's gone to London. Molly loves him but if he only thinks about himself, about going off to chase his dreams, she'll marry Mike. Remember that, Brucie.'

*

When the song ended and the clapping stopped, Uncle Reub said, 'Let's find the pig races.'

We walked over to the track, but as we approached Uncle knew something was wrong. The track was empty. Pig racing was on weekends.

'Nerts!' he shouted to himself then after a few seconds he turned to me. 'I thought you'd love pig races. They're so much like dogs. I'm sorry I got the dates wrong.'

'That's OK,' I replied and my uncle suggested we go over to the midway.

The home-baking tent was on the way and we stopped there hoping there might be something to eat but there wasn't. The baking was for show only and the two of us walked around all the baking on the periphery of the tent then around the large table in the middle.

'Mrs Nichols is too modest,' Uncle said, pointing to a gold ribbon. 'She's won the top prize for her butter tarts. Now that she's won, she won't mind if we take one.'

'You can't do that,' I said. 'They're for show, not for us to eat.'

We walked on to the midway, where my uncle bought me a large cone of pink candy floss. On one side of the midway there were sideshow tents with a fire eater, a sword swallower, a knife thrower and a man in a turban who lay on a bed of nails.

'They use secret tricks don't they?' I said confidently to my uncle.

'The real secret is there's no secret to what they do. Each one has learned to do what he does. It's dangerous if you or I try it but not for them. Shall we watch?'

'No. Not if it's not dangerous. Let's go see the animals. They're more interesting,' I replied, and we continued down to the cattle barn. I loved watching Mr Everett's cattle eating clover in the fields. I thought it was beautiful how their bodies swayed as they walked along the highway back to their barn. That summer I knew I wanted to spend as much time as I could just watching animals, and in the show barn I might have a chance to actually touch some.

'Howdy, doc,' I heard someone say as we neared the black painted barn and it was the vet who treated Angus.

'Dr Smith! I shouldn't be surprised to see you here today,' my uncle replied.

'Work and pleasure. Work and pleasure,' he said.

Today he looked neat as a pin, in freshly ironed, light brown bibbed overalls, a dark green shirt and a brown wool tie. His black rubber boots had manure on them.

'Working for the Agricultural Society today. Can't be too safe about infectious diseases.'

'Are you, as it were, the gatekeeper?' Uncle asked and the vet explained that at the crack of dawn he was inspecting the livestock in every single truck and trailer arriving at the fairgrounds.

'Rabies is on the up too. Any critter that looks dumber than it should doesn't leave its trailer. Wish you could do the same for polio. At this time of year I worry about taking my kids on the train.'

'There's a promising polio vaccine being tested in Pittsburgh,' Uncle told the vet. 'In this fresh air I'm not worried about my nephew. Are you going to the judging?'

'Nope. My hard work's done. I'm the fireman now,' he replied, 'here if I'm needed. Good to see you. Say, doc, as you're an eye specialist, I wouldn't mind your checking my left eye some time. I'm seeing a different colour with it.'

'Is there any difference at night?' Uncle asked.

'Yeah, if I close my right eye I see haloes round the lights. If I squint they're still there.'

'You might have a cataract,' Uncle said. 'I've got my ophthalmoscope at my sister's. If you can get out to Lake Chemong I can take a look.'

'I'll see if I can do that,' the vet replied and we continued into the barn.

Cattle judging had been taking place all morning and the Peewee class – for boys under ten years old showing their senior, intermediate and junior calves – was under way. I thought the calves were the most beautiful I had ever seen. There wasn't a speck of manure on a single one and their coats shined fresh and clean like Angus when he was wet. Each boy walked his calf through an entrance to the ring at the left and out an exit to the right. Most of the boys walked with their heads down. I thought that's exactly what I would do. Grace wouldn't. She'd strut right into the ring and look at everyone in the eye. One boy had a particularly pretty red calf. Most of the calves were Herefords or shorthorns or Angus but this one was different. She had the most enormous brown eyes and bleated with a surprisingly high voice when she was walked through the ring.

My uncle and I stayed for almost an hour then left and visited the food tent where we both had hamburgers, French fries and Vernors ginger ale. I saw Mr Everett come in, order food and leave.

'I don't know why he's here. He hates animals,' I whispered to my uncle.

'I agree with you. He's not a nice man. Country folk only ever meet their own kind. That's what makes them so suspicious.'

'He killed his dog without asking anyone if they wanted him.'

'Between you and me, he's simply a stupid man,' Uncle replied.

'My dad would have taken his dog.'

'I'm sure he would but Farmer Everett only sees dollars and cents in animals. A bullet is cheaper than dog food.'

'Giving him away is cheaper than a bullet,' I responded, and my uncle nodded in approval.

When I had finished my lunch my uncle asked me if I would like to see all the Agricultural Society winners. The owners would be auctioning some of them, mostly to other farmers wanting to improve their stock.

We returned to the cattle barn and I couldn't understand a word the auctioneer was saying, he was speaking so fast, and at first I found it hard to tell who was bidding, until Uncle Reub told me to watch the men in the first four rows. Almost all of them wore denim overalls and railroad engine drivers' striped hats. They were the main bidders and if you watched carefully you'd see them nod their heads ever so slightly. I didn't recognise any of the successful bidders, except for Mr Preston, the butcher on George Street Mum occasionally bought steaks from. He bought an enormous Aberdeen Angus.

I hadn't expected to see the pretty red calf ever again but, just as we were about to leave, it was walked into the ring, this time by a grown-up.

'Wait,' I told my uncle. 'Let's watch.'

The bidding started and I thought I saw Mr Preston the butcher bidding for the calf.

'We must buy it!' I whispered to my uncle.

'We can't,' Uncle Reub replied as the auctioneer continued his high-pitched chatter.

'We must! The butcher will kill it,' I whispered, and still looking straight at the calf I shot my right arm high in the air and held it there.

'We can't bid,' Uncle Reub said once more but I disregarded what I heard and kept my hand held high and the auctioneer continued his fast-talking.

'Put your arm down. You're underage and they won't pay any attention to you,' Uncle Reub said. And as he spoke he raised high his left arm and kept it raised.

'Sold to the man in the bright shirt,' the auctioneer proclaimed looking straight at my uncle and me.

'Now what do we do,' Uncle said, as much to himself as to me.

'We give the calf back to its owner,' I said firmly.

We left the spectators' stand and Uncle went to the cashier's desk, wrote a cheque, was given a receipt and told to collect his livestock before the end of the day. While he did that, I wandered through the spectators asking the farm boys I met where the owner of the red calf was. I asked the boy himself without recognising him and told him to go outside the back entrance of the cattle barn and to wait there. I had a present for him.

'Found him!' I shrieked with glee to my uncle at the cashier's desk. 'You get the calf and bring her to the back entrance. I'll meet you there with her owner.' And I raced off to stay with the calf's owner until my uncle brought the calf to us.

Uncle had to pay extra for the halter the calf was wearing. He told me later he was pleasantly surprised at how readily it followed him from its stall down the corridor to the back entrance, then remembered it had been trained from birth for showing. Outside the back entrance I was telling the boy about our new boat.

As my uncle approached the two of us, with triumph in my voice I said, 'Here's your cow back!'

'Don't want it,' the boy replied. 'Got another.'

I leaned forward and stroked the calf's head.

'It's your friend. She's pretty,' I replied.

'Got me a better one,' the boy answered. 'Is that the present?'

'Yes,' I said.

'Thanks, but no thanks,' replied the farm boy, and he turned and walked back into the barn.

I watched my uncle's shoulders visibly drop, then ever so slowly they gradually went back up.

'Bruce, you're a good boy,' he finally said to me. 'That was very generous of you. But perhaps we should sell the calf to the butcher.'

'No! He'll kill it and cut it up,' I replied.

'Did you enjoy your lunch today?' Uncle responded.

'That's different. I didn't know the cow the hamburger was made from. It wasn't red with brown eyes.'

We both settled back into our own private thoughts. Mine were all sad, that the farm boy didn't love his calf anymore, that Mr Preston wanted to kill it, that hamburgers were made from such gentle animals with so wondrously enormous eyes. I'm sure my uncle was thinking about what we could possibly do at the end of a Thursday afternoon, in Peterborough, with a cow on a leash. Then, I don't know where the idea came from, but I knew exactly what we should do.

'Uncle Reub, let's go back to the ticket booth and ask Mrs Nichols if Mr Nichols is here.'

'What are you thinking?'

'We give Mrs Nichols the calf to grow up and become her milking cow. And Mr Nichols takes it back to their farm. May I tell her?'

Uncle beamed at me. 'Of course you may. Brucie, you may think you're just a small boy but inside you're something else. You're a real mensh, you're a man.'

MRS NICHOLS'
NEW COW

A t first Mrs Nichols refused to accept the calf but then Uncle
Reub explained exactly what happened and that she would
be doing him a great favour if she took the calf off his hands.
With a twinkle in his eye he told her that if she couldn't find it
in her heart to help him out of his predicament his only other
option was to arrange then and there for a calf roast for all the
remaining visitors to the Ex. Then Mrs Nichols explained that
her husband wasn't there and that she was returning home
with the Everetts in their car, and again we didn't know what
to do, but this time my uncle had the answer.

'Do you think Dr Smith is still here?' Uncle asked and Mrs
Nichols told him that at this time of day the vet would be in
the Agricultural Society office in the black barn. She said she'd
go and see and came back with him.

'Howdy, doc. Hello, son,' he said. 'So I see you'd like to go into farming.' He stroked the calf's neck.

'Fine animal. Feed her right and she'll grow like the blazes. Mrs Nichols tells me you'd like her to look after her.'

'That's right, vet,' Uncle replied, 'but I was wondering, if you have the time, whether we could kill two birds with one stone as it were.'

'How's that?' the vet asked.

'Your hospital is only a few minutes away and am I right in assuming you have a livestock trailer?'

'Yes,' the vet replied, with hesitation in his voice.

'If you could help us get this calf to Mrs Nichols' farm, that's only a few minutes from my sister's cottage where I have my medical equipment. I could examine those eyes of yours and give you a diagnosis of what's happening. Professional courtesy of course.'

'Sounds good. I'll be back in a snap,' he replied, and he was, in his green GMC pickup truck towing an open-topped wooden box on wheels. He lowered the trailer's back ramp, walked the calf in and tethered her to a ring at the front end of the trailer.

'Four in the front's a squeeze,' he said. 'Son, you travel with your calf in the trailer. My boy loves that.'

It was bumpy at first, leaving the fairgrounds, and I had to grab onto the top of the side of the trailer to stop myself from falling over, but once we were on paved roads everything was fine. When I stood my head was just above the top of the trailer, only a few feet above the truck's cab, but driving up Water Street, with the river on my right, Peterborough looked completely different. So did the countryside. Everything looked bigger, brighter, fresher. On the straight highway to Bridgenorth the vet drove as fast as my father did. Mum said that was too fast but I loved the wind in my face.

At Mrs Nichols', we unloaded the calf and took it to an empty stall in her barn. I'd never been inside and although it was almost dusk I could see that it really needed a good cleaning. While he was there the vet examined her two cows and had a quick look in her chicken coop, then we said goodbye to Mr and Mrs Nichols and drove down to the cottage.

'Hey, Angus. Got in any tussles lately?' the vet said to my dog as Angus greeted him. Mum looked surprised to see him there and her brother said, 'Dr Smith here was in our neck of the woods and I thought I'd give him a quick eye examination. I'll explain everything later.'

Uncle Reub asked Mum whether she minded him turning off the lights in the living room and while she made tea for them, the vet sat in the dark in the higher of the two rocking chairs while Uncle Reub asked questions and examined the vet's eyes. I was surprised how many questions he asked, how long it took and how close Uncle Reub had to get to the vet's face to carry out his examination. Uncle Reub asked the vet to cup his left eye then his right eye and, holding up fingers, asked the vet how many he saw.

After he finished he said, 'Well, sir, the retina, lens and vitreous of your right eye are all normal, but I'm afraid you have a maturing cataract in your left eye and it will get worse.'

'Jesus, does that mean I'll go blind?' the vet asked. He sounded frightened.

'No, you'll never go blind but you might eventually lose the sight in your left eye. You can adapt. I know surgeons who keep on operating with unilateral cataracts.'

'What about removing it?' the vet queried. 'Will that help?'

'Not much today but in ten years it will. There's an eye surgeon in London, England – my age – who during the war noticed that RAF pilots with cockpit canopy splinters in their eyes didn't reject the splinters. He's having good results replacing cataracts with Perspex lenses.'

I listened in and thought what my uncle was saying was just amazing, that doctors could do such things. The vet stayed for dinner and the two men swapped stories about what they did. Because the vet was there I was allowed to stay up late. After he left I told Uncle Reub that it was the best day of the summer.

'For me too,' he replied.

'I bet it won't be as much fun when we all go back on Saturday.'

'It will be as much fun as you make it, Brucie,' Uncle replied.

Before I went to bed I walked through the vegetable patch, past the gull and the dog, into the wild field behind the cottage to where it met the woods. Fireflies silently turned their lights on and off and I wished I had taken a jar with me. As I watched the sparkling display, I saw a flashlight approaching and thought it was Mum coming to tell me it was time for bed, but it wasn't. It was Uncle Reub.

'I thought you'd be here,' Uncle said.

'I was just thinking,' I replied.

'Maybe that's why I enjoy your company so much,' Uncle responded.

He sat down with me.

'Do you remember I told you how Indians have different names throughout their lives, the first one the mother gives, then later ones that a father or uncle gives after they've gone on their first successful hunt?'

'Yes.'

'Well, Brucie, you know I sometimes call you Brucie and sometimes call you Bruce but from now on you're Bruce. Bruce, you went on your first successful hunt today and, by gum, you bagged yourself some impressive game. Do you know anyone else your age who successfully bought a cow at auction?'

We both grinned wide.

'Bruce, because of your successful hunt today, you are no longer a boy and I claim the right, invested in me by God, country, the wolf cub pack, your family and as your uncle, to give you an appropriate new name.'

'Do you mean "Bruce"?' I asked.

'Yes, you deserve a grown-up name but you are entitled to a special name.'

Uncle stood to attention and faced me.

'Bruce, forest rangers look after the woods. But the animals of this world they need someone to look after them too. I hereby name you and forthwith you will be known by all asunder as "Beast Ranger".'

Uncle reached forward, grasped my right hand, gave me a firm handshake, and a salute. Then he clasped his hand on and off his mouth giving war whoops, turned, and still war whooping followed the light from his flashlight back to the cottage. I giggled and followed him. As we walked inside my nostrils were filled with the aroma of fresh baking.

Mum walked over to me and gave my head a soft caress. 'Mrs Nichols tells me that peach pie is just for you.'

COLD RAIN

I pulled the covers over my head and listened to the soft wind bind the cottage in a cold Arctic hug. That evening, all of a sudden, it was dark before bedtime. The air felt different. It was bleaker, with a menace. At night the cottage was wrapped in a damp grip and the next morning a cold fog threatened. Then it rained, freezing rain for days and I knew summer was over.

Just as I could smell the warm south invading the lake in early summer, I could smell the cold north that was testing to see what it could do to the cottage in the coming winter. That freezing wind, winter's scouts riding down the lake from the north, was looking for the first trees to paint with frost. Water squeezed and trembled on the cottage's windowpanes. A poplar bough beat itself against the side window, jangling the loose panes of glass in it. While the rain and wind played their duet, whitecaps charged down the lake and the waves beat like tom-toms on the beach, each wave sucking at the rocks on the foreshore. The line of poplars on the road behind the cottages bent down trying to touch their toes. The far side of the lake was lost in shifting curtains of gunmetal grey. It was horrible weather and somehow utterly beautiful.

There was nothing to do in weather like that but to stay in the cottage and keep warm. Mum burned logs in the fireplace all day. Grace and her sister and Rob and I played crokinole and Monopoly and cards. We read Hardy Boys books and listened to the crackling radio. We talked and we argued and then we got bored and decided to go over to Grace's bunkhouse to see if there was anything more interesting to do there. Grace went over to my uncle, who was reading. 'You can come too,' she said.

The wind was too fierce for him to use his umbrella so he wore my dad's waterproof army poncho as we walked over to Grace's cottage.

In the bunkhouse the girls got on their beds and Rob and I sat on the bearskin rug on the floor. Uncle sat on the chair next to the window. The electric heater had been on all day so we felt cosy and warm.

'I hate this weather!' Grace spat out, to no one in particular.

'It is miserable,' Uncle commented.

It was Grace who asked Uncle to tell us another Sioux Indian story.

'Do you want a long or a short one?' Uncle asked and we answered, in unison, 'A short one.'

'How do the Indians remember their really long stories?' I asked and Uncle said, 'Where people don't read much, their memories are better than ours.

'Now then, this story is about the wind coming down the lake today,' Uncle began. 'The Sioux believe that the north, south, east and west winds are really spirits and all of them are brothers.'

'Why not sisters?' Grace asked.

'That's an interesting question, Grace, and you'll learn why soon. Once upon a time the North Wind and the South Wind and the East Wind and the West Wind all lived together, in the far north, at the North Pole, in the land of the Northern Lights and sky ghosts. They were, as I say, all brothers.

'The North Wind was the oldest brother. He was cold and stern, a bit like Clarence Everett. The West Wind was next oldest. He was strong and made lots of noise, Robert and Bruce, somewhat like your father with his hammer and saw. The East Wind was the next son, actually the middle son because there were in fact five of them. He was always cross and angry. A bit disagreeable, like Jebediah Sweeting can be sometimes. The South Wind was next and he was the second youngest, always pleasant and very agreeable, like you, Bruce.'

'Iris is always sweet,' Rob interjected in a sing-song voice but this time I remembered what my uncle had told me, that strength didn't come from your arms or legs, it started in your head then spread slow but sure to the rest of your body, and I said absolutely nothing. I didn't even look at my brother, and our uncle continued.

'The brothers paid no attention to their youngest sibling. He was the Whirlwind. Always full of frolic and silliness, much like you, Grace.'

'I'm not silly!' Grace pouted. She didn't like being called silly.

Uncle Reub continued, 'The North Wind was a great hunter and he got immense pleasure from killing things.'

'Like Mr Everett killed his dog!' I said.

'I'm afraid so,' replied my uncle. 'On the other hand the South Wind hated killing things. He preferred to make and grow things.

'The West Wind usually helped his South Wind brother make things but not always. Sometimes he sided with the

North Wind. The East Wind was simply lazy and always tried to get out of having to do anything.'

'Let's call him Perry,' I said. Grace giggled.

'The Whirlwind, well he was like a puppy dog. He never had anything serious to do so all the time he played and danced. Sometimes he played in fields and made dust devils. Sometimes he danced on the lake and made water funnels. All the Whirlwind ever wanted to do was have fun.'

I looked at Grace and her eyes were now dancing with delight. She always saw dust devils and waterspouts before I did and stopped whatever she was doing until long after they had disappeared, always hoping they might suddenly return.

'One day, a beautiful woman came to the brothers' home. She was so beautiful, so utterly breathtaking, all of them, every single brother, except the Whirlwind who was too young to understand the power of beauty, almost fainted when they gazed on her. She was that beautiful. After seeing her nothing else mattered. That's what happens with men. They could only think of the beautiful woman and each of the brothers wanted to marry her.'

'Do you mean sleep with her?' Grace asked, but her big sister told her to keep quiet and listen, so Uncle continued.

'Women understand the power they have over men and this beautiful woman was clever and wise and knew she could ask for whatever she wanted from the brothers. So she told them to show her what they were capable of doing and she would choose as her husband the one who pleased her the most.'

'That's how Mum picked Dad,' Rob injected. 'She had him build a cottage for her.'

Uncle Reub continued.

'The North Wind was absolutely confident that with his power and strength he would please her the most. He went hunting and brought back game for her – massive moose and meaty deer and fat geese and ducks, but because the North Wind was so cold and ruthless, everything he brought back turned to ice, and when he brought the game indoors their home became cold, and dark and lifeless.

'The deafening West Wind beat on his drums. He sang and he danced and thundered and stomped on the earth, but because he was so flamboyant and loud and noisy, the house fell down, just like a farm in a Kansas tornado.

'The lazy East Wind, well he did nothing at all. He just sat down and talked and talked, mostly about himself, about how happy he would be if he ever married, about how contented he would be, knowing he didn't ever have to look for a wife again, about how pleased he would be, knowing that the beautiful woman was his. This bored the beautiful woman to tears. She felt like telling him to stop thinking only about himself and make something of himself.

'Now the South Wind, he did exactly what you'd expect such a thoughtful brother to do. In the warm rays of the morning sunshine he searched for ravishing flowers for her. He gathered raspberries and blueberries. He built a fireplace in the home, gathered oak and cedar boughs and cut them into logs and made a roaring fire for her. He turned their house into a warm and bright and comforting home. The beautiful woman saw that the South Wind had done all of this for her and with a quiet and still and loving smile on her face, the radiant woman said she would marry him.'

We sat in silence, captivated by Uncle Reub's story. I wondered if there would be a happy ending or not, not knowing whether this would be one of his stories that suddenly meandered off in a different direction.

'Well, the news that this fragrant beauty would marry the South Wind annoyed the North Wind enormously and he got very angry. He told the beautiful woman quite bluntly that as he was the oldest brother, and the strongest, and the most powerful, that she should marry him. The other brothers all disagreed and even though he was their elder, the West Wind and the East Wind both sided with the South Wind and the three of them decided to leave the North Wind and move away from the North Pole.

'The West Wind moved to where the sun sets each day, beyond the forest across the lake from us. The East Wind moved to where the sun rises each day, beyond the elms and white pines behind the cottage. The South Wind, to get as far away as possible from his strong and powerful big brother, moved as far in the opposite direction from the North Wind's home in the Far North as he could go, far, far beyond the bottom of Lake Chemong. His kid brother, the sparky little Whirlwind, well he didn't have a say in anything because he was so small, so he tagged along with the South Wind although sometimes he stayed with the West Wind. He never stayed with the East Wind because that brother was no fun at all.'

'Is that how the wind got to come from all directions?' I asked.

'It is, but the story continues and now it gets unpleasant. So they all left the North Pole, but as they departed the North Wind bellowed like a wounded bear and declared to his brothers that from that moment on he would forever fight them, to get even with them, and first of all, to get his revenge, he would turn the beautiful woman and her dress into rock hard blue ice.

'"I will destroy beauty!" he roared.'

We sat in rapt attention. Grace leaned forward so that she didn't miss a word.

'The North Wind exhaled his freezing breath all over the beautiful woman,' Uncle went on, 'but the gorgeous lady's dress was magical. As the North Wind blew his icy air over her and her dress turned to ice, it became larger and larger and larger. It spread all over the earth and it protected her from being frozen to death by the evil North Wind.

'Now, all the land was completely covered by the beautiful woman's icy dress and her husband, the South Wind, could not see where she was. He called out to her and she answered from beneath her dress, but because it had spread so far she could not find her way out from under it and the South Wind could not find any way to get under it to rescue her.

'So the South Wind went to his brother the West Wind for help. They breathed their warm air on the dress, and as they warmed it, beads on the beautiful woman's dress shone and sparkled in gorgeous greens and vibrant reds and striking yellows and brilliant orange. It was really something to behold. The little Whirlwind thought he was helping but he wasn't. He just skipped about all over the dress, throwing things in the air, but his playful antics made the South Wind and the West Wind smile so they worked harder. The East Wind helped a little at first but then he said he was tired and he stopped.'

'Just like Perry,' Rob commented.

'By the end of the day, the South Wind and the West Wind were completely exhausted and they both fell into a deep sleep. While they were dozing the North Wind returned and he froze the dress once more, making it hard and lustreless and cold. All the colourful and beautiful beads and ornaments that shone brightly during the day again became dull and covered in shards of ice. The little Whirlwind saw what his biggest brother was doing and tried to wake up the South Wind and the West Wind but they were so exhausted from their hard work they wouldn't awaken. The little Whirlwind woke his brother the East Wind who, with considerable coaxing, was persuaded to go and help but he helped just a little and then sat back down. His real plan was to see who might win then take the side of the winner. Some people are like that.

'When they awoke the next morning the South Wind and the West Wind saw what their elder brother had done overnight. Together they drove him away and once more they started warming the dress, but that night the North Wind returned again, embraced the dress and froze it once more, keeping the beautiful woman trapped beneath. So the South Wind and the West Wind had their work to do all over again and soon the beads and ornaments on the beautiful woman's dress yet again shone with light, but the North Wind returned that night and all over again froze the garment on top of the earth, destroying its beauty.

'Children, this went on, day after day, then year after year and eventually generation after generation, a relentless combat between the North Wind and the South Wind helped by the West Wind that has continued ever since. No one ever wins. It's become an eternal struggle. That's what's happening outside this bunkhouse right now. In the coming months the North Wind will think he has won, that he has destroyed the exquisiteness of the beautiful woman and her gorgeous dress, but come spring the South Wind and the West Wind will overcome their brother once more, at least for a time, and the jewels and beads and ornaments of the beautiful woman's gown will appear as herbs and flowers and shrubs and trees, as bushes and mosses everywhere. The beautiful woman will become mother to the earth but just when the good brothers think they have won, the North Wind will revive once more. That's Canada. That's what this country is.'

Uncle's story and the rain ended just about together. It was as if the South Wind and the West Wind had been listening but when we all went outside, although the sky was clearing now there was a fiercely cold wind blowing from the north, so cold you needed a sweater and coat. We went down to the lakeshore to see what damage the storm had done, but I decided I wanted to stay with Uncle Reub. I had a different question to ask him.

Walking back to our cottage I asked my uncle, 'Do you think Grace is beautiful?'

Uncle replied, 'Yes she is. Why do you ask?'

'I like being with her more than with Rob or Perry. They might think I don't like them if I play with Grace instead of them.'

'Here's a thought then,' Uncle said. 'A great joy is just thinking about what you think is beautiful. It doesn't matter what other people think. If you want to know if something's really important, you can close your mind to other things. Just shut your eyes and everything else is gone and what's important is even bigger. Try that, Bruce.'

We stopped and in the crisp, fresh air that surrounded us I shut my eyes and soon everything was gone from my mind except the most important thing and I said, 'I don't want the summer to end. I want it to stay.'

Uncle paused for a moment.

'Bruce, I'm taking the Dayliner back to Toronto tomorrow. I've decided to re-open my medical office.'

'Why did you close it?' I asked.

'Because when I shut my eyes, what I thought was most important really wasn't.'

'What was most important?' I asked. Uncle Reub looked at me, straight into my eyes.

'I'm told my son is now a doctor in Boston,' Uncle replied quietly. Then he continued, 'Will you see Grace in the city after you've gone back?'

'Do you have any more children?' I asked, after a long pause.

'No,' was the reply.

'He doesn't live with you?' I asked.

'He did when he was young but after I separated I didn't see him or his mother.'

'For how long?' I asked.

'He was around your age when we divorced. Then I married again, and separated again.'

My uncle put his hand on my shoulder.

'Beast Ranger, if my son is willing to see me I don't want to embarrass him.'

GRADUATION

It was the last Tuesday of August, our final swimming class, but today wasn't a lesson, it was graduation. After we took our swimming tests the previous week, Mrs Blewett sent invitations home with us, inviting parents and friends to a picnic on the marina lawn, followed by a demonstration of synchronised swimming, and then the awards ceremony for those of us who passed our swimming tests. She was the test examiner and all summer I'd dreaded my test. I was completely relaxed sculling and treading water. I didn't have any difficulty watching where Mrs Blewett threw a linen sugar sack with a round granite rock inside it into the lake for me to duck dive, find and carry on my chest back to the dock. I was good at my breaststroke, sidestroke and backstroke and mediocre at my back crawl, but I just couldn't do a good front crawl. I breathed in too much water with my mouth.

Rob splashed a lot when he did the crawl but it was his favourite stroke. Perry was practised and fluid. Grace was like a muskie. When she did the crawl she wasn't just fast, there was hardly a ripple in the water. Everyone was faster than I was. But when I'd taken my test last week, the day was warm and the lake like glass and I was, if I may say, pretty good.

The day before, our two mothers went into Peterborough and stocked up on hot dogs and buns, mustard and relish, serviettes, local Macintosh apples and freestone peaches from Niagara. We drove to Bridgenorth in Grace's mother's car, Grace's family in front and, with Uncle Reub back in Toronto, just Rob, Mum and me in the back. Steve and Perry's mum brought them and joined us on the lawn.

Mr Blewett had embedded posts on the grass and hung red, white and blue bunting over the lawn. A Union Jack flew from the flagpole by his house and a Red Ensign from the flagpole by the shoreline. It was a real party.

We picnicked together, Grace's family, Perry's family and mine, and while the mothers gossiped, Mr Blewett and his teenage son roasted our hot dogs on the barbecue and brought them to us when they were ready.

'Your brother was very positive when he came over to say goodbye to me and the girls,' Grace's mother told my mum.

'Yes, I was surprised. He walked all the way up to our cottage to say goodbye to my boys,' Perry's mother added. 'He's charm itself.'

'He certainly is,' my mum replied. 'When he stops dreaming and thinking only about himself he's the most fascinating man I know.'

'He told me I should chase my dreams,' Grace said.

'Well, he told me I should look around me and be content with what I've got, exactly what I've been telling him all summer!' my mother replied, and I heard a tenseness in her voice.

'He told me the same thing,' Grace's mother said. 'He said that what he learned from watching our families is that we have everything: good health, good husbands, good children. He said, if only our grandparents could see us.'

'Before he left he asked Morris to go for a walk with him. Imagine!' said Mum. 'When I asked Morris what Reub wanted to talk about, he said Reub asked for help setting up his office. He's doing that right now. But they talked about other things too. I'm sure of it. When they returned from their walk Morris kissed me and he was already at the cottage. And then he asked where Bruce was and said he was going to take him fishing.'

I knew exactly what day she was talking about because I was amazed that Dad had asked me to go fishing without someone telling him he should. Now I knew why.

I wanted to listen to more mother talk, it was interesting, but Mr Blewett announced on his megaphone that the ladies were ready to do their synchronised swimming display. All of us walked down to the floating docks, sections of the old floating bridge that acted as a barrier to protect the boats in the marina. There was Mrs Blewett, the postmistress; the lady from the general store; Mrs Bell the garage owner's wife; and three more women I didn't recognise all in blue bathing suits and white swimming caps, all with nose clips on, all lined up facing us, all 'buxom'.

'Girls, about face,' Mrs Blewett said and they all turned clockwise and faced the slightly choppy lake.

'Three, two, one, go,' I heard her say, and simultaneously they dived into the lake, as gracefully as seven plump cormorants, not a splash from any of them. For the next ten minutes, the ladies of Bridgenorth gave us a display of synchronised swimming. They treaded water, then in unison disappeared, to reappear in a circle with their right arms raised high. Like spokes on a wheel they did overarm backstrokes, then back dives, and surfaced with all of them throwing Mrs Blewett straight up in the air. They sculled upside down with only their legs above water, like upside down fat parsnips in a bucket of water. They somersaulted. They duck dived and reappeared in a straight line of white bathing caps, linked by arms on their neighbours' shoulders. Watching them swim, having such obvious fun together, I realised that the locals weren't only there for us during the summer. They had their own interests and got on with their own lives, even when we invaded for the summer.

After the display, Mrs Blewett towelled herself down, took off her bathing cap and, using her husband's megaphone, invited us all up to receive our badges and medals. I was given my Intermediate Red Cross badge. So were Grace and Perry. Rob and Steve got their Senior Red Cross badges the year before, this year they were awarded their Royal Life Saving Society bronze medallions. In just a few years Rob would become a summer lifeguard at the lakeside park on Water Street in Peterborough and I'd become a Red Cross Instructor, helping Mrs Blewett at the marina in Bridgenorth.

CLOSING THE COTTAGE

Closing down the cottage was always a sombre and protracted event. On those days at the very end of August, my parents never smiled. They spoke little and when they did their sentences were short and brusque. Do this. Do that. That's wrong. Hurry up. Don't stand around. Not like that. Don't pester. The weather didn't help. On the day we were leaving, whitecaps rolled with menace on a black lake. They hit the shore and their power blew foam and strands of seaweed across the sand, into the spearmint and onto the cut grass.

The day before, Dad had cut the grass for the last time, then he'd harvested every single cucumber and tomato in the vegetable patch, even the green tomatoes. Mum would pickle them with dill. He pulled the remaining carrots but left the beets. He'd harvest them on a later visit. His watermelons were the size of footballs but when he cut one open it was yellow-white inside so he left the rest. I knew he hoped that somehow they would ripen before he returned. They never did. After everything was picked, Dad covered the exhausted vegetable beds with banks of seaweed Rob and me wheelbarrowed up from the beach. He carried everything he didn't want to the fireplace on the front lawn – pieces of lumber, cardboard boxes, newspapers, magazines, plastic buckets, all the surplus remains of summer, poured gasoline on it all, struck a match and in an explosion of flames, all those useless remnants turned to carbon.

All day my parents busied themselves. Everything store bought, the tent, the lawn chairs, the tackle box, the garden tools, the water buckets, the axe, the crowbar, the sledge hammer (so heavy I could hardly lift it, but my father could swing it over his shoulder and crash it down on a stake with one hand), were brought into the cottage or the tool house or the bunkhouse.

Along the point and the highway, red and yellow leaves had suddenly appeared, first on shrubs and now on single branches of maple and birch trees. There was no song in the air, but high in the sky hundreds of birds whirled in tight black flocks drifting towards the causeway and beyond to the south. I thought they were leaving because, with everyone going back to the city, the lake was no longer a happy place to be.

Without my father asking, I decided to help stack the remaining firewood under the cottage while Dad oiled his saws and his vice and his pliers and stored them in the tool house.

'Robert, you and Bruce bring the canoe and put it on the horses,' our father told us and I felt good, that my dad thought I was big and strong enough to do a grown-up's job. When it came to the rowboat, Rob and I carried one end and Dad the other, as we lifted it from the beach onto the grass then tipped it on it back, put a sawhorse under one end, then another under the other, and tied a tarpaulin around the boat. We tied another tarpaulin over the canoe, and in their brown shrouds both boats looked like giant slugs resting on green beds.

Dad raised the motor on his new boat, then pulled the boat by its stern rope around the front of the dock and manoeuvred it backwards into the boathouse, but he didn't raise it out of the water just yet. He would be returning on his own on weekends until the fishing season ended.

On the day of our departure, just before leaving, Mum pulled all the curtains shut. During the summer, closed curtains made me feel cosy but now they made the cottage lost and lonely. I watched and I thought she was drawing the curtains because the cottage had died and summer was no longer alive. It was like the end of a movie at Mr Yudin's theatre. Dad opened the damper on the fireplace flue a little, in case it rusted shut over winter.

The station wagon was loaded and Rob was already in the back when I said, 'Wait,' and I ran past the vegetable patch to the split cedar fence where the sweet peas grew, picked all the pink flowers that remained, and brought the bunch back to the car.

'OK,' I said.

Dad started the engine and we left for the city.

Grace had gone back to Toronto earlier that day. I thought I might give the sweet peas to her when I got there but I didn't. I didn't see Grace again until the next summer.

A LATE VISIT

In early November, my father returned to the cottage one last time and I was surprised that without my mum telling him to, he asked me to come along. When we got there we were greeted by Reg Muskratt.

'Bit sharp,' Mr Muskratt said as Dad and I got out of the car, and it was. There had been a hard frost overnight and the mounds of yellow poplar and red maple leaves that clothed the lawn like discarded summer clothing were still sparkling and crisp.

I did what I always did when I got to the cottage. I raced around to the front to look at the lake and, although that morning's honey-coloured sky had turned Caribbean blue, the lake looked cold, unfriendly, alone. There wasn't a single boat on it but our old boat, now Mr Muskratt's, was tied to the dock. Dad had written to him, asking him to come down to help winch the new boat out of the water and up into the boat-house for the winter.

Dad could have asked Mr Nichols or another father visiting the point that weekend to help him, but he'd asked Reg Muskratt. Just as I appreciated why my father planted the poplars to hide the red brick house from his view, I was now aware why he asked Mr Muskratt to help him. Everything about Mr Muskratt, even his name, said 'country', and it was in the lakes and forests that my dad felt at ease with life. Reg Muskratt personified what my father really wanted to be, part of the natural world. Perhaps that was one of the reasons why he was a florist, not a huckster like some other dads.

Frost had wilted most of the leaves in the vegetable patch, leaving a constellation of plump pumpkins nestling on the earth, and in that soil there were footprints from large animals. They must have been deer prints but some were so large I wondered whether a moose had visited the vegetable patch. I thought about what Uncle Reub had told us, that when we left and returned to the city the animals took back their land.

I collected the five largest pumpkins in a pile beside the station wagon, to take back home for Mum to make pie. I left the watermelons, they were soft and rotting, but I harvested the remaining beetroots. I went up to Mrs Nichols' and she showed me how well the calf had grown.

'I call her Ruby,' she said, and for a second I thought she'd named the calf after my Uncle Reub. Maybe she did.

Eating the cookies she gave me, I walked up the point. The road and the cottage lawns looked like they had been sprinkled with confetti and I felt like I was walking through a carnival, what with the colours and the musty smells. What I saw made me smile – jewels and beads and ornaments like on a beautiful woman's dress.

'They didn't give up!' I thought and I felt as defiant as those leaves. Then I remembered another story Uncle Reub had told me about why leaves fall, that the grasses and herbs had no protection from the cold, but just when they thought they couldn't survive any longer, the leaves from the trees came to help them, spreading like a warm blanket over their tender roots, offering a thick warm rug against the chill of winter. The Great Spirit saw how generous the leaves were, giving up their lives to protect the grasses, so he gave them vibrant red and yellow and crimson colours to make the rug as beautiful as possible.

When I got back to the cottage, Mr Muskratt and Dad had taken the big white motor off the boat, hung it from a wooden stand Dad had made for it in the tool house, and were winching the boat out of the water. They had slung chains over rafters in the boathouse, then under the bow and stern of the boat, and both men were pulling in unison on the chains. I saw the chains strain against the wooden hull and wondered why the men had not done anything to prevent the damage I was seeing to the splashboards.

In less than an hour they had completed their task. The two men stood quiet on the dock, content with their work, then Mr Muskratt said, 'Some fishin'?'

Dad said, 'Sure.'

His eyes danced. He'd always wanted to know where Mr Muskratt fished.

We got rods, reels and lures from the tool shed and headed down the lake in Mr Muskratt's boat, stopping near the shore where Grace and I had buried the heron. Mr Muskratt anchored there.

Mr Muskratt used a jointed red-and-white wooden surface lure with two sets of triple hooks. Dad and I used similar lures but ours were green and black on top, white underneath.

'What happens if we catch fish and the police catch us?' I

asked the grown-ups. The fishing season for everything except perch and sunfish had ended.

'I'll tell 'em it's my catch,' Mr Muskratt answered. Then he turned to my father. 'Mrs Muskratt tells me to ask after your brother-in-law.'

Dad replied, 'He's fine. Opened his doctor's office. Good to have him back.'

Then a silence descended on the boat for a while until Mr Muskratt asked, 'Gonna be a fisherman when you grow up?' and I told him I'd like to be a forest ranger.

'Seasonal work,' he replied, and we continued fishing.

My father cast his lure from the bow, Mr Muskratt cast from the stern and, being especially careful with my casting, I fished in between them. I looked at the men and they were no longer the Lone Ranger and Tonto, they were twins. They didn't look the same. Dad wore a thick brown coat and his trousers were dark gabardine, warm enough for trips to the North Pole. Mr Muskratt wore bibbed denim overalls under his red-checked lumber jacket. I thought they could be twins because both seemed so completely at ease in their own silence. So did I. In that silence the only noise was the whip of our lines being cast, our lures hitting the water and the soft purr of our reels as we slowly wound them back to the boat. Then Dad said, 'I thought you wanted to be a doctor when you grow up?'

'I did,' I answered, 'but I'd like to spend time outside with animals and that's what forest rangers do.'

'Don't spend time with animals. They work for Lands and Forests spotting forest fires,' Mr Muskratt interjected.

'Then I'd like to be a vet,' I said. 'Uncle Reub says they do everything he does but he just looks after people and vets have to look after everything else.'

'Good income,' Mr Muskratt added.

*

I never expected I would be the only one to catch a fish. When the bass struck, my rod bent almost in half.

'Let it out,' Mr Muskratt commanded and I let the bass run with my lure.

'Reel slow,' he said and I started to bring the fish towards me.

'Out,' he said and I stopped. And so it went on, for five minutes, then ten, then fifteen. When I fished with my father there was always a greater urgency to catch the fish.

'Patience, boy,' Mr Muskratt advised, something I never heard my father say, and after twenty minutes the tired bass was near enough for my dad to get a net under it.

'Good fish,' Mr Muskratt said, as we examined the bass flipping about in the net. He took a small wooden truncheon from the bottom of the boat, hit the fish on its head, it quivered for a minute then it was still.

'Good trophy,' he said, and I looked at my father and saw sunshine sparkle.

'Reg, do you think the taxidermist will do it at this time of year?' Dad asked, and Mr Muskratt replied, 'Money always talks.'

I was so proud I caught that fish. I wanted to show it off to everyone but more than to my mum, or Perry or Rob, or even Uncle Reub, the person I wanted to show the fish to was Grace. I hadn't seen her since the day we left the cottage at the end of August and now, on the lake, I really missed her.

On the afternoon we left the cottage at the end of August, while I was stacking the remaining firewood under the cottage, Grace had run over.

'We're leaving now so goodbye,' she said.

'I thought you were going tomorrow,' I replied.

'Daddy's going tomorrow. I'm going today with Mummy,' she answered.

'Will I see you in Toronto?' I asked and she answered, 'I don't know.'

Then she kissed me right on the lips, said 'Bye' and ran back to her cottage. It was nice, her kissing me on my lips, and I thought about that for a bit, but then I just got on with packing up.

Each August summer at the lake ended this way. I didn't want to go but I did. Angus didn't want to go but he did. Grace and I didn't want to stop seeing each other but we did. That's just the way it was. I'd wished I'd said more to her, that I'd kissed her back.

My father had that largemouth bass I caught, close to four pounds in weight, mounted on a cedar plank. He hung it on the wall of the cottage and to this day the first thing we see when we open the cottage door is that fish. Until that summer, really until that autumn when he brought that bass back from the taxidermist, I didn't know that you might be silent but that didn't mean you didn't think, or didn't love. Under the fish's white belly, on a shiny brass plaque screwed into the varnished cedar there were words.

'CAUGHT BY MY SON BEAST RANGER. THE BEST FISHERMAN ON LAKE CHEMONG.'

POSTSCRIPT

Uncle Reub returned to medical practice, where he moved from eye, ear, nose and throat into psychiatry. He married one of his patients, and when she died he had a further nervous breakdown. In his final years he lived in a nursing home. Perry, who became a publisher, was a constant visitor. Steve graduated in law and moved abroad, first to Switzerland, then to Costa Rica.

Rob initially managed our father's flower business. He became and still is a jazz disc jockey. He and his wife, Melissa, took on the responsibility for maintaining the cottage.

The Blewetts sold their marina and in later years over-wintered in Florida. The Nichols continued living in their farmhouse, but gave up farming. Dr Smith continued working as a vet. The hospital he set up is now 100 per cent small animals.

In 1964 Mud Lake Indian Reservation Number 35 became the Curve Lake First Nation Territory. A few years later, the Whetung family opened the Whetung Ojibwa Crafts and Art Gallery, now one of the largest galleries of its kind in Canada. The annual powwow continues. The indigenous families, the Muskratts, Whetungs and Coppaways continue to live and work at Curve Lake.

My father continued to spend all his spare time at his cottage. In his latter years, he and Mr Everett became mellow friends. My dad remained robust and healthy until he died at ninety-seven years of age. My mother, now a hundred years old, continues to visit the cottage each summer. She just scored 99 per cent on a cognition test, better than any of her children or grandchildren.

I became a veterinarian. My parents thought that because of the length of the course I should become what they called 'a real doctor'. Uncle Reub spoke with them on my behalf, saying it was a noble choice and one for me to make. After graduation I found myself in London, England, where I stayed, married and had children. Until they were in their teens my kids spent every summer at Lake Chemong. My son, Ben, now a writer and television presenter, says his summers at the lake were the most formative experiences of his childhood. My parents' grandchildren now take their kids to the cottage.

I lost contact with Grace fifty years ago.

If you have enjoyed this book and would like to find out more about Bruce Fogle or our other authors, please visit www.septemberpublishing.org and follow us @SeptemberBooks.

September is an independent publisher; curating, collaborating and championing.

B